G000099229

DREAMS

EDITORIAL NOTE

In 'Dúiche', Anna Ryan Moloney's radiant and meditative essay for this book, a connection is mapped between architectural and personal space, between the built and the emotional or spiritual environments, the territories of memory and meaning. It is a particularly resonant approach to writing about a university, a place where lives are altered, memories are formed and meanings are investigated and contested. 'Dúiche' means 'hereditary land' or 'demesne'. The present offers a good moment to put together a chart of the demesne, to assess the sustainability of what we have and to plan for what we'll be passing on.

This volume marks the fiftieth anniversary of the University of Limerick (UL). It presents fifty contributions from or about people associated with our university. As with many maps, the individual elements are often beautiful or striking, but the effect is best experienced by stepping back to take in the totality.

'Dreams' is the title of a widely loved song by The Cranberries, a band whose connections with UL are strong, as founding member Noel Hogan and local music promoter Ber Angley make clear in this book. The contributors we selected were asked to take the word 'Dreams' as a starting point and offered a maximum space of 1,300 words per piece. Beyond that, we made some suggestions as to theme, but no editorial proscriptions.

The writings range from scholarly essays to students' tweets, through poems and presentations, to personal memoirs and transcripts of talks. Loretta Brennan Glucksman's foreword recalls major funding and development initiatives on the part of her late husband, Lewis, and their friend Chuck Feeney. The president of Ireland writes about the passionate socialist for whom our business school is named. A student journalist portrays with affectionate gentleness the Library Café's 'Pink Ladies'. Donal Ryan, the most consistently excellent Irish novelist of his generation, contributes a brilliant short story that might also be read as an eco-parable – a fitting read for those of us whose days are becalmed by our riverside workplace.

Voices in the assembled chorus of this book include those of current under-graduates and alumni, retired professors, members of the catering and grounds staff, sportspeople, musicians, artists, nurses, diarists, researchers, chroniclers, visitors, teachers, seekers and campaigners. A different trio of editors would have made a different selection (as would any one or any two of the current three), but our hope is that the book offers contributions that would be included by every editor wishing to reflect the vividness and diversity of UL life in the early 2020s.

The University of Limerick, the first university to be established since the foundation of the state, came about through determined local campaigns – as remembered in this book by Paddy Meskell of the inaugural 1972 class and by Bill Whelan, internationally acclaimed composer of *Riverdance* – and, later, through the merging of the National Institute of Higher Education and Thomond College of Education. The story is told in David Fleming's assiduously researched study *The University of Limerick: A History* (2012), and in found-ing president Ed Walsh's lively account *Upstart: Friends, Foes and Founding a University* (2011). Our own book is not a chronology but a conversation that builds into a characterisation. The fifty pieces may be read in any sequence, from cover to cover, or dipped into.

The reader will notice the emergence of resonances, rhymes, repeated themes, preoccupations. Research. The Glucksman Library. Sport. Music. A respect for creativity. An affection for colleagues. Our students as our teachers. The beauty of the campus. The image of the Living Bridge shimmers through a good many of the pieces – an actualised metaphor for teaching, learning and outreach – and the Shannon flows in reflective counterpoint. But a current of iconoclasm is at work in these writings, too, a restlessness, a desire to push onward. There is often a commitment to engage with communities in wider and more welcoming ways, to make an impact on more lives, to do more around the major issues of class, gender, identity, disability (or '"dis"ability', to borrow a trenchant term of orthographic subversion used by our contributor Charlie Mullowney), environment, marginalisation, exclusion and participation. While there is great pride in these pages, there is ambition and activism too. The powerful words of Sindy Joyce, Denise Chaila and Donnah Sibanda Vuma are reminders that much remains to be done; that everyone has a right to safety, freedom and education; that protest matters; that real inclusion and diversity will make us all stronger. A closer relationship with Limerick city is seen as a matter of pressing importance and the opening of the UL City Centre Campus as an exciting opportunity. These priorities are what make UL the place it must continue to become: a university where there are beautiful buildings but no ivory towers.

We extend sincere thanks to our wonderful contributors for their willingness to participate and for their skill, also to Wendy Logue and Conor Graham at Irish Academic Press, and copyeditor Dermott Barrett. We thank Gobnait O'Riordan, Kate Harris and Ken Bergin at the Glucksman Library, Carla Capone, Rina Carr, Yvonne Cleary, David Fleming, Oonagh Grace, UL President Kerstin Mey, and Caroline Keane and Cliona Donnellan for assistance with contractual matters. We add our thanks to UL Confessions administration, and to Eoin Brady and Michelle McMahon, Dr Eimear O'Connor, Sorcha Pollock, and UL Fifty Programme Manager Caroline Rafter. The late David Lilburn, artist, cartographer and designer, was a much-loved UL creative presence for many years; we thank his wife, Romanie van Son, and Yvonne Davis (whose fine essay on UL's art collections appears in this book) for helping us to include an example of his beautiful work.

FOREWORD

Loretta Brennan Glucksman

In 1984, Lew and I began our great Irish adventure with our first trip from New York to Ireland. We landed in Shannon and were driven to Adare where we stayed at the Dunraven Arms. Seàn Donlon, the Irish Ambassador to Washington and a valued friend, had a dinner party for us at his home in Killaloe. It was a magical evening and truly set the foundation for so many wonderful events that would form our next decades in Ireland. Ed Walsh, president of UL, was there of course and invited Lew to come to campus the next day and speak to a class in the Business School. The rest, as they say, is history.

Lew knew Chuck Feeney through business, but there was a shared goal when they realised the amazing extent of possibilities to develop with UL. This of course was music to Ed's ears. They proceeded to structure and to strengthen the UL Foundation (ULF), to direct the significant amount of funds they intended to raise for several new projects. We soon met Gerry Boland, an astute fiscal and political professional who worked closely with J.P. McManus, who also later became a cherished friend. We would come to rely greatly on his generous and savvy view on local and national issues. Another early friend and counsellor was Dan Tierney, a successful businessman who was also intent on fulfilling the huge potential of UL on a fast track. I have great memories of terrific executive sessions of the ULF board across the street at the Castletroy Park Hotel.

As our interest and exposure to UL increased and we met further interesting and convivial people, we began looking for a house in the area. Again through UL, we met Gordon Holmes, a respected local attorney, who became our wise counsellor and dear friend. So many other people we met remain our friends today, including notably Michael Houlihan and Eamonn Cregan whose lovely families we saw grow and prosper.

Gordon managed our purchase of Ballyneale, a beautiful old Georgian home on the Newcastle West Road, just half an hour from UL. That was our wonderful base through seven happy years in Limerick, until the call of the sea and his beloved boat once again summoned Lew and we moved to East Cork. Gordon was managing partner of the law firm, Holmes O'Malley Sexton. With the elegant synchronicity that blessed all our time in Limerick, Harry Fehily, current head of that firm, would take over as Chair of the UL Foundation. Harry is now my valued link to the important working of the board, especially as we have been so restricted in travel for the past few years. Jim McCarron was a friend and, indeed, physician to both Chuck and Lew, and he joined the board also. Jim and Maureen became essential elements of the ongoing work, triumphs and great fun we all had at UL.

Chuck and Lew and several more of the early enthusiasts were keen to expand student residence capacity on campus and quietly set about purchasing large blocks of property on both sides of the Shannon. I have wonderful memories of the redoubtable John O'Connor negotiating with the good nuns on the Clare side of the river. A personal treasured UL experience was the building of Brennan Court Guest Accommodation. My father, William Brennan, was

a wise and kind man who had six years of schooling and was also one of the most successful people in my life. Lew's naming of that essential building for my dad is one of the most glorious gifts he could ever have given me. The magnificent Irish World Academy of Music and Dance, state-of-the-art academic and residential buildings, and the beautiful symbolic link of the Living Bridge all pay homage to the diligence and generosity of the dedicated people who would not give up.

Chuck had been working on building a world-class concert hall on campus to bring international artists to Limerick and help showcase the brilliant musicians that were being drawn to Limerick by another UL genius, Mícheál Ó Súilleabháin. The University Concert Hall attracts audiences from all over Ireland. It is also an architectural gem that is the perfect counterpoint to our beloved Plassey House.

In the beginning, there would be a great, convivial dinner in the dining room at Plassey following the board meetings. The food and wine were lovely, but the conversation was spectacular. Although Chuck and Lew loved the fun, neither was a late-night guy. So, they developed a system to recognise who could graciously (very relative term) leave the party first. On learning the next day who got out first, the winner had to send the guy who stayed a new tie. Lew had quite a collection of beautiful ties sent with compliments by Chuck.

Lew believed that the library was the beating heart of any centre of learning, and he loved the library at UL. But he had hopes of expanding its footprint and adding the burgeoning technology increasingly available. The stunning edifice on the UL campus is just beyond his greatest dreams. It was a long way from his first initiative at the library when he asked to add a space where students could read current newspapers and magazines in order that they were learning within a context of up-to-the-minute facts and opinion. It was an innovation in the training programme he had introduced at his beloved Lehman Brothers, where he spent most of his very fulfilling career on Wall Street.

I am humbled and elated to introduce this book of Dreams, to celebrate all the accomplishments that UL has wrought, and to dedicate ourselves to carrying on helping the leaders and the students of UL into their continuing glorious future.

Dr Loretta Brennan Glucksman, a former chairman of the Board of the UL Foundation, is a leading figure in global philanthropy.

THE KINDNESS OF LIBRARIANS

Sheila Killian

he first thing I loved in UL was the library. Not the gorgeous piece of architecture we have now, but the original – a low-ceilinged, possibly windowless, open-plan room at the top of A-Block. It was all shadowy stacks of books and journals, always warm, smelling of dust and coffee, with timid graffiti done in biro on the dark desks.

At that time, I had no right to be there. I was a trainee accountant in a big firm in Dublin, with a boyfriend in Limerick. The job was fine but seemed a little pointless. People were going places and I thought I was going there too. They were taking out loans from Anglo Irish Bank, buying shares in film schemes, eyeing up the property pages. The money train was boarding, my friends were climbing on. I had a first-class ticket, but I was hanging back and didn't really know why. And then study leave – weeks off work to study for the professional

accounting exams, so I hot-footed it to Limerick, to hang out with the boyfriend and his buddies. I only came to the National Institute for Higher Education (NIHE) to find a place to study.

Library security seemed to be poor enough to let any chancer without a student card just walk right in. Nobody stopped me at the door. It was quieter than most libraries, more anonymous, a place where you could drift and dream a bit. There were lots of accounting and auditing books, some of which surely helped with the exams, but there was also English literature – Beckett's plays, Eavan Boland's poetry and all those accessible first year texts in psychology and sociology, a tasting menu of ideas. The room was full of words and possibilities, few of which related to tax management or the corralling of wealth.

Librarians moved like monks between the shelf stacks, wheeling trolleys of books to be sorted. I watched them enviously. It seemed like the ideal job – spending all day in the company of books, caring for them. I imagined becoming a librarian instead of a tax accountant, in the same way a kid imagines working in a pet shop, erroneously and impractically, mistaking the proximity of the desired thing (books, rabbits) for the chance to enjoy them. Still, it was more than just wanting an escape from timesheets and capitalism – there was something else in the library that took a long time to identify, that made me feel at home.

One morning, a small queue had formed outside the library door. People were being asked for their IDs. I walked past anyway, to a smile and nod from the librarian as she asked the people behind for their student cards. Security wasn't lax at all, I finally realised. It was just that the librarians had correctly tagged me as harmless, perhaps also as cold and in need of shelter, and let me study in the warm room as long as it wasn't too crowded. It was kind.

Years passed, and I moved out of practising accounting, finally getting to work in UL full-time and spend all the hours I wanted among the books and journals. It's come up in the world, our library. Now it's housed in a beautiful steel and light creation with ingenious machines that pull books from the archives, comfortable spinning chairs in primary colours and dozens of gorgeous

nooks and crannies in which to read and write and think. The whole campus, in fact, is objectively more beautiful than it was in the 1980s. New buildings have sprung up on the far side of the river. There's the playful Royal Baking Powder visual echo of the medical school, the Hobbiton curves of Allied Health, and the fabulous gold and mosaic of the Irish World Academy of Music and Dance. And the river itself is lovely, teeming with life and reflecting the seasons, pouring under the wobbly Living Bridge. We have the best campus in the country.

But that's all just setting. It's the stage on which we move, and it would be beautiful and empty if that were all there was. The thing that makes the place special, the memorable thing, is people. The Irish World Academy building, for many of us, will always in our heads be called the Taj Mícheál, bringing memories of the cheerful genius of Mícheál Ó Súilleabháin, the vision he made real there and the way he always had a warm word for everyone. The anomalous panes of clear glass in the bottom level of the library carry a coded memory of the generous brilliance of Dave Lilburn, another man who carried his talent and his art lightly and gave his time to anyone who needed it. They were gifted, both of them, and they were kind. It's the kindness that warms our voices when we speak of them now.

Kindness is what makes the plaza coffee shop special too; the women who work there probably do more for the mental health of the whole UL community than any government initiative. It's kindness that makes Cruinniú, the staff trad music group, a welcoming place even when you show up with a tin whistle and more enthusiasm than talent. Kindness is Teach Fáilte laying on tea and biscuits for a group who are bereaved. It's kindness that has students holding doors and porters lending you umbrellas, or a colleague stepping quietly in to pick up the pieces when things go wrong. There's a lot to love about UL, but the best things aren't citations or rankings, validating and important as these might be. It's not the river, the Living Bridge, or even the stunning library building with its fantastic collections and beautiful books. Less tangible than any of these, and more important, is the openness of the campus to strangers and chancers and refugees from accounting firms, the generosity of colleagues, the laughter of students, the people we get to spend our days with, the kindness of librarians. These things make memories that matter and endure. And that's what makes the place special.

Associate Professor Sheila Killian is Director, Principles for Responsible Management Education, Kemmy Business School. Her first novel, Something Bigger, *was published in 2021.*

SOCRATICALLY PIGTOWN

Damien Thompson

You showed me how to do long division, and it only took the weekend to set me straight. Dawn 'til dusk with no time for Mass, thanks Ma. You opened my eyes to Yeats and Hopkins, taught me to trust my gut, your duty all ended Mr Noonan. Enjoy the ride, Bill Hicks, you wrenched open my brain ushering in freedom and truth. Prince Rogers Nelson, you showed me joy in repetition and beauty in every day. That last pair never graced Limerick, but Bob Dylan did and he's got a Nobel Prize, as does my old neighbour Kieran Carey (the first person I ever saw in a band T-shirt, guruing down Daly Avenue in U2's *Under A Blood Red Sky* – how can you wear a thing like that in a town like this?). Peacekeeper Kieran, we still can't quite believe how far you've made it and how big an example you've set for us. And Damo Dempsey is down here regularly, teaching us all the shit they don't in schools, not least to throw back our shoulders. The rain falls hard on Pigtown but that don't make us humdrum. No, we fire on our parkas and breakdance in the puddles. We love the rain, it helps us grow. My fellow CBS Sexton Street alumnus John Philip Holland went and invented submarines. How do you like that for making lemonade? It's a watertight example of the good things that can happen when a Shannonsider goes deep. Perched at the edge of Europe, we've got soul, no metal hearts in Mid-West Hibernia.

And to the scientist's children who will never receive a satisfactory explanation for why the sky is grey, I can only tell you I'm struck dumb by the purity, love and truth you wear. Go ask your beautiful mother for God's sake, she's the real teacher. I'm a research scientist working on IMPORTANT THINGS. I have no time for your juvenile miscellany as I map out what an atom is thinking. Spoiler alert: the atoms know nothing, nada, centre of a donut, zilch, they can't love you back (and it's too late to stop now). Atoms are unaware and amoral, not like us cleverest of animals – Huxley said apes can talk but don't for fear they'd be put to work. Here in the physics department at UL we're putting those atoms to work, and when they complain we call it getting excited, being promoted up into a higher state. How's that for humancentric propaganda – free the atoms, or maybe not. They love sticking together, can't help themselves. It relaxes them, bonding to form molecules, coalescing in a warm communal energy sink. Among many other useful and interesting things, this collective eventually birthed us great big lumbering behemoths, united nations of atoms, all-singing all-dancing assemblies of nanomachines, top-of-the-food-chain-evolved hunters and gatherers festooned in white lab coats, thrilled with ourselves as we unearth one more tiny piece of an infinite puzzle. Like dogs trying to perform card tricks, we never give up even when it's clear we should. Creating drug crystals atom by atom on a computer as we try desperately to reroute our biological pathways, all invaders must die. Sometimes we get fed up of wanting to live forever and take those crystals and zap them with lasers before welding them onto circuit boards (we're going to need more Blu Tack, Professor!), howling as we throw the switch. Adding some life to our years. Then having the *amour-propre* to report in sobriety that our hypothesis proved correct when in fact we were as surprised as you were when the little atoms started pulsing like a synthetic brain and whispering as an anharmonic oscillator (for the non-specialist that's a wonky mouth organ, we'll find a use for it).

Down here in Limerick we don't fear discordance, not a bit of it. Out here on the perimeter we know a confluence when we see one, and we bathe in it. William Brooke O'Shaughnessy, reared here by the majestic Shannon, stowed his intravenous drips and sailed to India, treating cholera and prescribing cannabis for muscle spasms (say nothin' kid). In his downtime he developed the telegraph system. For craic. Not bad for our little Limerick/Luimnigh/loimeanach sat on 'a bare marsh', or maybe 'a spot made bare by feeding horses'.

The years they run away just like those ravening ponies but leave in their wake an entrenched appreciation for the city's three proud bridges, the fabulously banjaxed Black Castle upstream of the UL campus, the lifelong love of learning that pervades all Shannonsiders, even the Limrockers, Treaty Stoners, eejits and gowls – you know who you are, we can smell our own. We all tumble in constant flux, searching and delighting in our history as we traverse our medieval city lined with Georgian townhouses, our shared rain-drenched streets. We see it, feel it, own it, proud products of our environment. From the triptych Dolores O'Riordan mural guarding King John's Castle to the Jewish graveyard watching stoically from the suburbs, it's all ours, our wedge of the rock hurtling around the sun at thirty kilometres a second in what we fear might be an otherwise empty universe. So let's nestle a bit closer together and support each other a bit more, yeah? We're all alive at the same time, all in it together, whatever it is we've found ourselves in. Sermon over, class dismissed.

Schooled in CBS, then UL, Damien Thompson modelled proteins in Paris and shrank circuits in Cork. He lives by the river with Sarah and their children, Luke, Jude, Hanna and Abbie.

HOPE AND MERCY

Kerry Neville

What brought me to Limerick and University of Limerick as a Fulbright Scholar in 2018? Fate. In 2017 I gave a reading for Narrative4 in Limerick, which is also the city where my great grandmother, Annie O'Connor, was from, before she emigrated to the United States in 1914. Through that event, I met Joseph O'Connor, who asked me to be a part of the Frank McCourt Creative Writing Summer School at New York University's Glucksman Ireland House that year and then supported my Fulbright Fellowship, offering me a place in the UL Creative Writing programme. Beyond these initial facts, I couldn't have imagined a better community of writers with whom to make a temporary (though permanent in memory) home. Sarah Moore, Donal Ryan, Martin Dyar, Rob Doyle and Eoin Devereux welcomed me into the fold, as did the faculty and staff in the

School of English, Irish and Communication, as did the UL students.

Since I didn't have a car, I walked almost everywhere, every day and across three seasons, through Limerick city and campus and beyond. Each walk revealed something new and complex and surprising. UL's Living Bridge swayed as if a tightrope suspended across a valley and I usually stopped mid-bridge to watch the herons paused on a rock outcrop as if they were students contemplating the metaphysics of the river. Each week, I walked past the enormous antlers and skull of a giant extinct Irish elk that hung outside my classroom at Plassey House and reminded me that a relatively new university (at fifty years) was anchored across the millennia to a beautiful craggy, boggy, ancient world that still kept its secrets.

Most days in Limerick, my temporary and beloved home, I was inside grey skies, a grid of buildings, and strangers under hoods and umbrellas who could be friends but were not yet. We rushed by in our haste to get to other places, to get warm and dry, to get food and drink, to get drunk and laid. But since I also lived across the street from the Shannon River, I wandered the boardwalk every day, with a vagabond's hope for a heron or swan to claim me, swooping me up in its broad, powerful wings across waters. As the Shannon is a tidal river, I tracked its rise and fall, and its current, quiet or quick, and understood, in my river keeping, the predictable metaphor: time was a current.

The Celts called the river Abha na Sionainne, for the goddess Sionann, daughter of Lodan Luchair-glan of the Tuatha Dé Danann, who went to the river in search of magical hazel nuts, cnónna coill, source of wisdom and poetic inspiration. Of these nuts, Yeats writes, 'I went out to the hazel wood, / Because a fire was in my head'. Because a fire was in her head, Sionann drowned, and by pagan transubstantiation became the river, forever dwelling in Tír fó Thuinn, the land under the waves. So, the river was a natural and supernatural current, a sacred betwixt and between that required patience for what was coming into my view.

My days were transformed by walking, waiting, wondering, considering, hoping and remembering that there was a world that existed beneath the waves

that I could not see. Each morning, rain or shine, though more often rain or rain, I settled with a coffee on a bench and marvelled at the riotous gulls, or wandered down the boat ramp into the muck, ankle deep in it, observing what lived and drifted beside me, around me, through me. Mute and whooper swans, cormorants, ringed and golden plover, black-headed gulls, terns, mallard and pintail ducks, dragonflies and damselflies; and somewhere in the dark deep, salmon, smelt, pike, trout and eels. And further up and down the river or along its banks, bottlenose dolphins, white lilies, marsh pea, bird cherry, kingfisher, lapwing and otter. Once a month or before an incoming storm, flood barriers blocked my entrance to the boardwalk. Typical American, I hopped over them to get my daily fix of birds (*a fire in my head, burning, burning, burning*).

Once, on a dawn walk along the Shannon, I was startled by a heron pair that swooped low, just a few feet above me on the boardwalk. I heard their wings, the effort of their flapping. Whup … whup … whup … whup. Slow measured strokes as if sculling through the sky with feathered oars. The birds veered back to the water and flew on, intent on some other river-rock or marsh. Grace, instinct, and concentrated effort.

Almost every day, I walked my great-grandmother's first neighbourhood by the Milk Market trying to see what she, Annie O'Connor, might have seen, and what she never returned to see, then and now, there and here, through memory and imagination. At some point during my walk, I imagined walking in her very footsteps and listened for her ghostly footfalls inside mine. My great-grandmother grew up speaking Irish, which was the reason I was taking Irish lessons while on the Fulbright, so I could hear her voice echoing inside of me, feel her language move in my mouth, a music that was part of my blood and bones and DNA. I whispered the rudimentary names of everything I could name *as Gaeilge*: crann (tree), éan (bird), eaglais (church), leanaí (children), báisteach (rain), tuar ceatha (rainbow).

To that end, three mornings a week, I walked up Clancy's Strand, crossed Sarsfield Bridge, and then up O'Connell Street for Irish lessons with my eighty-nine-year-old teacher, Dónal O'Ceallaigh. Dónal always waited for me with the front door open and would say, 'Dia duit! Conas atá tú? An raibh siúlóid mhaith agat?' (Hello, how are you? Did you have a good walk?)

'Dia duit,' I'd reply. 'Tá mé go maith! Tá sé ag cur báistí ach álainn.' (I am good. It is raining but beautiful.)

At some point on my walks, inevitably, I would cry. My great-grandmother grew up desperately poor and at sixteen, she bought a ticket in steerage on the *Titanic*. At the last minute, her parents decided she was too young to emigrate alone, and so she sold that steerage ticket to someone who, in all likelihood, died in her place. It is for this unknown passenger that I, raised Catholic and now mostly agnostic, pray on my walks through Limerick. Two years later, Annie O'Connor left on the steamship *Celtic*, arrived at Ellis Island, then worked as a nanny for a wealthy family in New York, and met her husband, William Lunn, an immigrant from Wicklow who worked as a chauffeur. She never returned to Limerick or Ireland. I was five when she died and my only memory of her is sitting at her feet in her tiny walk-up apartment in Astoria, Queens, while she crocheted colourful squares for a never-to-be-finished afghan and served me tea with milk and sugar, and Danish butter cookies from the tin.

There were times I could have dropped to my knees along the Shannon's boardwalk, the river that was the reason for the city, because I was so moved by this convergence. Full circle: there I was, on my own in Limerick, as she was when travelling to America; I was returning to her city in her place, for her. Her courageous journey is why I have had a life of privilege, not without my own sufferings, but a life far better than her life in a crowded tenement across the street from a pig slaughterhouse on Palmerstown Street. Could she have imagined all that her solitary journey would offer to her descendants? So, I was in Limerick and at the University of Limerick as a writer, a scholar and her great-granddaughter, trying to honour the sacrifice she made in leaving all she knew and loved.

On Sundays I walked from Clancy's Strand and across Sarsfield Bridge to St Michael's church, just a few streets over from her first home. Irish Mass, a service entirely *as Gaeilge*. I tried to pray inside Annie O'Connor's voice, within her voice, which had travelled across a century and an ocean back home to Limerick. I prayed for light and love and hope and mercy, and in full gratitude for my own journey home and away and home again.

Professor Kerry Neville, co-ordinator of the Creative Writing Programme at Georgia College and State University, was a Fulbright Scholar at UL in 2018. Her books include Necessary Lies.

SHARING A DREAM: CHAPLAINCY AT THIRD LEVEL

John Campion and Sarah O'Rourke

We are members of the Salesian congregation, inspired by the vision of Don Bosco and Mary Mazzarello, prophets of compassion and ministers of hope and joy, whose legacy tells us they were weavers of relationships, believers in the inherent goodness and divine destiny of every person. As educators they listened empathetically to those they encountered. They took an interest in the circumstances of their lives, thus allowing people, especially the young, to find their innate potential. For Don Bosco, 'Relationship is at the heart of education.' Mary Mazzarello advised, 'It is necessary to study the individual character and to know each one so as to succeed well and inspire confidence.'

The poem 'God's Dream' by the French poet Charles Péguy (1873–1914) makes a whole lot of sense when we pause to reflect on chaplaincy at Third Level:

> I myself will dream a dream within you …
> It is my dream you dream,
> my house you build,
> my caring you witness,
> my love you share;
> and this is the heart of the matter.

As chaplains, it is this dream of God that is the heart of the matter. This leads us to wonder in what ways we can live out this dream of God on a university campus with 16,300 students and 1,700 staff.

Strategic to the operation of UL Chaplaincy are the purpose-designed Teach Fáilte and Contemplative Centre on the campus. They afford the chaplains space to offer opportunities for worship, provide welcome, pastoral care and support, to facilitate spiritual engagement and reflection, to encourage social responsibility and volunteerism.

Teach Fáilte is a centre of welcome and hospitality, located in the Student Square. It is the face and the hub of the chaplaincy services. Our presence as chaplains there is key to the implementation of our mission of being a holistic, inclusive service aimed at the authentic development of the human person for students and staff of all faiths and none.

Chaplaincy provides a listening service that responds and reacts to the ebb and flow of life, whether that is a tragedy and loss or joy and achievement. Teach Fáilte attracts over 500 students weekly. This high number is due to the eclectic services found there, including a safe home-away-from-home atmosphere and facilities for UL students and staff; space for students to chat, get to know each other, exchange stories of the ordinary and not so ordinary, and support for students who need encouragement as they navigate their way through the academic cycle. Our chaplaincy also supports activities and events such as the UL President's Volunteering Award, which includes the opportunity for volunteering in liturgical ministry, social media administration and as meet-and-greet hosts. As part of this award, all volunteers complete a reflective portfolio.

Its greatest value lies in the pastoral care and counselling bridge it offers to vulnerable students who may not seek help elsewhere. The chaplains are very aware that the presenting issue is not always the key one for which the student needs support. These include coping with bereavement, loneliness, family concerns, relationship breakup, addiction, sexual orientation, chronic illness, financial difficulties, seeking asylum and a more general search for meaning. In times of difficulty, students are assured of a non-judgemental listening ear and may be facilitated to avail of other supports on or off campus.

Owing to Covid-19 restrictions, the chaplains were unable to provide the hospitality of the boiling kettle, but remotely we continued to provide the hospitality of listening. Some students found it difficult to adjust to online learning and others felt socially isolated. Many missed face-to-face contact but appreciated the space to be listened to over the phone. From experience we know the wisdom of the Gaelic proverb, 'Giorraíonn beirt bóthar': two people shorten the road.

Staff and students are encouraged to avail of the Contemplative Centre, which is an oasis of peace and tranquillity. This is a sacred space for quiet meditation, prayer, reflection and Sacramental moments. It is here that people take time to open the Word of God and break bread. Throughout the academic year, bespoke interfaith and denominational services are held for special occasions of celebration or tragedy. It has been a long-standing UL tradition to host an annual remembrance service. During the Covid-19 pandemic, support to the bereaved from the wider UL community was not available as before. The chaplains, with the assistance of the president's office, the Irish World Academy and volunteer students, offered a virtual remembrance service. This provided a measure of consolation to those who were grieving and was an opportunity to collectively reflect and take time to remember.

The Contemplative Centre is also available for group gatherings and visiting speakers. Chaplaincy provides an Interfaith Directory where staff and students can meet people of varied faiths and traditions in UL and throughout the mid-west region. Interfaith calendars are on display in the Contemplative Centre as well as in Teach Fáilte. At present there are plans for a Memorial Garden as well as a larger prayer space for our Muslim community. All faiths can share and come together in the dream of God.

We continue to share a journey with those we encounter, and we walk with hope-filled hearts, ever mindful that we are sharers of a dream entrusted to us.

Chaplains Sr Sarah O'Rourke FMA and Fr John Campion SDB are an integral part of the Student Affairs Division.

THAT'S WHERE YOU COME IN

Carl Corcoran

S ammy Cahn, the acclaimed songwriter of the Great American Songbook era, penning songs for Frank Sinatra and others, once quipped, 'I am often asked, which comes first – the words or the music? I answer that what comes first is the phone call asking you to write a song.' I've been asked what inspired me to take on the role of course director of the MA in Songwriting at UL. Like Sammy, I simply answer, 'The invitation.'

After seventeen years of radio broadcasting with RTÉ, and having reached the age of sixty-five, I accepted the edict from the 'Suits' that my broadcasting career had come to an end. The parting from friends and co-workers was celebrated in a retirement party organised by my colleagues, to which many associates and contacts were invited. Amongst those in attendance were representatives of the Irish World Academy at UL, whose friendship and connections had been

nurtured over those years through mutual interests. Another connection that I had with the academy was my year of enlightenment when I took an MA in Community Music there. My friendship had deepened with the late Professor Mícheál Ó Súilleabháin. At that same retirement soiree in July 2017, Mícheál, along with then Director of the Academy, Sandra Joyce, and I chatted about the next chapter in the Corcoran biography. They asked if I might be interested in a role in the inaugural year of the MA in Songwriting. I can unashamedly boast of my interest and some prowess in the craft. A glimpse of my biography illustrated that I had experience. My passion for songs and their dissemination was palpable, and my affection for the Academy and those who work there was well known.

'Would I what! When do I start?'

'Tomorrow,' came the reply.

They say when He closes one door, He opens another. It seemed to me on that day, there was a whale of a draught blowing, with both doors open and a welcome hand reaching out from one of them. I grasped it tightly and rushed into the embrace of my soon-to-be-invaluable faculty colleagues.

The MA in Songwriting had been three years in the planning, with contributions at various stages from creative writers, academics, professionals, administrators and practitioners of the craft. The document handed to me on day one had much to absorb. It was a monumental and inspiring work and it begged the question, which I expressed to my director, 'How do you intend to deliver this aspirational menu?'

'Ahhh,' Sandra said. 'That's where you come in.'

And so began a journey that occupied and preoccupied, even consumed me for five years. I savoured the role of guiding, mentoring, sharing songs, and the craft of creating them, with enthusiastic, committed students, wide-ranging in age, ability, nationality and background. I revelled in the creative cauldron that is the academy building on the beautiful UL campus. I marvelled at the commitment and passion that my fellow faculty members displayed in their respective courses and disciplines.

But not only within the Academy – across the bridge too, within the UL community. Over the years, I arranged for contributions and collaborations with colleagues from Creative Writing, English and Sociology. All combined in a wealth of talent that infused my songwriters with the joy of creativity. I love this cross-pollination; this cross-faculty co-operation; this across the Living Bridge interaction. With the academy's rich tradition in arts practice research, our songwriters are afforded the opportunity to delve into the question of *why* we write – and in so doing, they inform their songwriting practice with a higher degree of self-expression.

A special pleasure was the interaction with the visiting songwriters who came and shared their process, providing insights into their approach and techniques. We all differ. There is no right or wrong way. Often, it was those conversations that were the most enlightening. In my radio career, and particularly in the last ten years when I presented and curated an eclectic mix in *The Blue of The Night* on RTÉ Lyric FM, I championed many great Irish songwriters who now reciprocated that support by accepting the invitation to visit the MA programme and spend a day with my students. Songwriters of the calibre of Lisa Hannigan, Eleanor McEvoy, John Spillane, Duke Special, Saint Sister, Bill Whelan, Emma Langford, Niamh Regan, Conor O'Brien (Villagers), Julie Feeney, Mick Hanly, Declan O'Rourke all shared their wisdom, and continue to do so. For this, I am forever grateful to them. I was also able to provide a performance platform for a lot of these visitors (until the pandemic brought that to a halt) by presenting a series of Sunset Concerts – live performances at the end of their busy day with the students, open to the public – attracting many audience members from the UL campus – another initiative that attracted footfall across the Living Bridge. I blossomed and thrived in the company of these creative individuals, both the visitors and my UL colleagues. Inspiration oozed from the very walls. The water-cooler conversations or the chats over coffee in Blas Café resulted in further investigation of the creative practice, and I, the supposed instructor, become the instructed. My own creative practice has been rekindled – how could it not be!

My next retirement is inevitable. But I am confident that, like before, I will be shepherded to equally rewarding pastures. What door will be opened? What hand will reach out from inside that door? As I emerge from these past five years, I acknowledge that I am more experienced, maybe wiser, confidently contented with a job well done and certainly enriched by the company.

After a distinguished career, acclaimed broadcaster, songwriter and teacher Carl Corcoran retired from UL in 2022.

IN THE LIBRARY

Mary O'Malley and Martin Dyar

A double sonnet on the opening of the new UL Glucksman
Library Building in 2018

In Athena's House

This house is domestic, safe for take-off.
Nooks, books, at the window the necessary wolf.
The mind opening meets his stare and worries
at its own thirst. A boy struts in, the man you'll marry.
The hunt begins. There are diversions. Heroes
with studs and tattoos that play to the audience.
The rasp of teeth on the back of your neck
reminds you of your purpose. It pulls you back.

Walls dissolve in the mind-altering spaces
among the quarks, the quincunx and gobsmack,
new stars greet old angels between June pages,
and from the floor along the stacks
a low growl as you fall softly on a thought
briefly disturbs the silence, your first rebel act.

Mary O'Malley

The Shannon Reader

Here are her timetable vows: one hour
at the river, then two in the library,
and then back down to the river again.
This rhythm bore no automatic fruit.
But a day came when suddenly the whole
thing sweetened and deepened. She found herself
on first name terms with concentration's ghost,
while currents kissed the root of every book.
She's upstairs now, the Shannon's own reader,
within whose work the otters see themselves,
the one whose silence manifests a line
heard on the bridge, a line the sun makes true
by changing these black words into a shoal:
I read, I write, therefore all life is near.

Martin Dyar

*Poets Mary O'Malley and Martin Dyar have both held the Arts Council Writer in
Residence Fellowship at UL.*

THE REDRESS OF MUSIC

Mícheál Ó Súilleabháin

(edited by Helen Phelan)

L et me begin by explaining my title: it contains the seeds of the core proposal for this paper. The Irish Nobel Laureate Seamus Heaney used the title *The Redress of Poetry* for a collection of his essays. Heaney proposed that 'consciousness can be alive to two different, some might say opposite, dimensions of reality and still find a way of negotiating between them'.[1] Heaney develops the idea of the crossing between opposing dimensions by referring to poet Robert Frost, who contrasts 'the children's house of make-believe' and 'the house in earnest', the actual house within which and out of which our day-to-day reality is worked through.[2] We might think of these houses as the extraordinary, lifting the ordinary out and over its mundane existence, and the ordinary grounding the extraordinary in the temporal.

This meeting of the extra/ordinary is captured beautifully by Heaney in the following words: 'We should keep our feet on the ground to signify that nothing is beneath us, but we should also lift up our eyes to say nothing is beyond us.'[3] He tells us that the course he was made to hold 'by temperament and by a decided consciousness, was the via media'.[4] What he is talking about here is what he also refers to as 'two orders of knowledge' – what he calls 'the practical and the poetic'.

> I wanted to affirm that within our individual selves we can reconcile two orders of knowledge which we might call the practical and the poetic; to affirm also that each form of knowledge redresses the other and that the frontier between them is there for the crossing.[5]

This idea of moving freely between 'two orders of knowledge,' of embodying both poeticism and practicality within the one person, of moving between the world of the imagination and 'the world in earnest' – between the playhouse and the farmhouse as Heaney has it – resonates with a new perception of binarism.

For example, is the Earth flat or is it round? It seems to have sufficient flatness to allow us to walk across it without falling off, but the horizon always moves away from us due to what we now know as the Earth's curvature. The new binarism is not so much an either/or as a both/and. It is not so much a discovery of something new as a new perspective on what has always been there. Biologist Anne Fausto-Sterling uses the metaphor of a Mobius strip to illustrate the notion of binarisms that bring each side into being together:

> The Mobius strip is a topological puzzle, a flat ribbon twisted once and then attached end to end to form a circular twisted surface. One can trace the surface, for example, by imagining an ant walking along it. At the beginning of the circular journey the ant is clearly on the outside. But as it traverses the twisted

ribbon, without ever lifting its legs from the plane, it ends up on the inside surface … [thus] as the image suggests, the inside and outside are continuous and one can move from one to the other without ever lifting one's feet off the ground.[6]

When the Irish World Academy building on the University of Limerick campus was being designed, I was struck by how aspects of the actual architecture of the building reflected the duality and movement between sides, implied by the Mobius strip metaphor. The main theatre, Theatre One, is located directly opposite forty doctoral research desks, as if to juxtapose the playhouse with the house in earnest. And it is the space between both houses that might be thought of as defining the essence of the academy itself.

This space is the arena where the performing artist walks freely between the playhouse of practice and the earnestness of research: between, if you wish, a search arising out of the need to answer and research contributing to the grounded reality of investigation and analysis. This model is not some kind of twin tracking of interests. Rather, it calls for an organic transformative interplay between the imaginative internal experience of practice and the external scientific application of logical thought.

The redress of balance between the poetic and the practical has its initial impact within the individual (the psychological) and subsequently may be applied to new concepts in other areas (e.g., education, social action, and politics). How might these reflections on poetry, philosophy, and binarisms, the production of knowledge, the space between the playhouse and the farmhouse, and the relationship between individuals and institutions play out in grounded ways?

In my own life, cultural mediation has manifested itself in both musical and educational spheres. I understand art as prophetic, as having a capacity to intuit happenings before the reality catches up. If a political or social movement might be enacted first through art, how might I work towards a sound that resonates with what I was, or with what I was becoming, or was to become? For me, answering this question demanded an engagement with different kinds of music and aesthetics … In my case, searching out strategies of cultural mediation that enabled classical and traditional musicians to perform together across the orality/ literacy divide was an attempt to redress imbalances that might exist between different voices, different traditions, different points of view. The suggestion here is that by setting a cultural imbalance right, any social or political imbalance might also be at least partially addressed.

In early Ireland, we find the utopic mythological figure of the hero Fionn mac Cumhaill and his band of warriors, Na Fianna. One of the central visions of Fionn and the Fianna was what was termed 'Cothrom na Féinne' (literally, 'the equality of the Fianna'), meaning the balance or equality that they required for fair play to be manifest. 'Fair play', a commonly uttered phrase in Ireland, might be a colloquial translation or equivalence in English. A more common contemporary translation is 'parity of esteem', and, indeed, this is the term used in modern legal terminology – the term 'Cothrom na Féinne' is used as standard in all Irish-language legal texts.

And so 'parity of esteem' sits beside the word 'music' in the subtitle of this keynote address. As does the word mediation. What I am suggesting here is that the process of mediation (the via media referenced by Heaney earlier) is a central one through which parity of esteem is addressed, where imbalance is tackled and where something is called out to allow a flow of energy that sweeps matters on, that unblocks progress and that frees up new healing levels of communication and shared endeavour. Mediation is a middle way, an acoustic that exists in the liminal space between perceived realities. It is literally the medium through which issues of injustice are addressed and put right. Our calling is in the arena of cultural imbalance, where certain voices are bypassed, for whatever reason. And more specifically, our calling speaks or sings of musical imbalance.

In my experience as an arts education activist, such imbalances may be viewed in two ways. One is as a problem to be solved. But another is as a missed opportunity. It is this latter perception that I find most helpful. The opportunity to question includes the unlocking of new voices previously excluded from the arenas of performance, education and cultural politics, among others. The presence of new voices demands what I might term a new listening, distinct from whatever system takes them in. The impact throughout the system is a rebalancing and redressing that is not only revolutionary and creatively subversive, but that is also sustainable. The process of redressing imbalances brings with it its own fertility of purpose and reward of opportunity and achievement. Again, in my experience, it is not only the newly arrived voice that benefits from this meditational action, but the entire sound community.

Notes

1   Heaney, Seamus, *The Redress of Poetry* (Faber and Faber, 1995), p. xiii.

2   Ibid., p. xiv.

3   Heaney, Seamus, *70th Birthday Speech* (Dublin: Irish Museum of Modern Art, 2009), p. 4.

4   Ibid.

5   Heaney, *The Redress of Poetry*, p. 203.

6   Fausto-Sterling, Anne, *Sexing the Body: Gender Politics and the Construction of Sexuality* (Basic Books, 2000), pp. 24–5.

Mícheal Ó Súilleabhain (1950–2018) was Founding Director of the Irish World Academy of Music and Dance. Helen Phelan is Professor of Arts Practice and Director at the Academy.

HE'S BEHIND YOU!

Sinead Hope

I took the helm at the University Concert Hall (UCH) towards the end of 2013, a time when the concert hall was emerging from another economic downturn, with plans underway to mark Limerick's triumph as European City of Culture for 2014. Not knowing a soul in Limerick or the region, I felt it was an opportunity not to be missed. One year turned into eight.

Hundreds of concerts and six house moves later, I continue to be in awe of the beauty of the city and region as well as the resilience of the arts community and indeed the wider community who continue to find new ways to showcase the character and soul of Limerick.

From week one, with eight *Riverdance* shows to be staged in UL's Sports Arena, to mark the opening of Limerick as City of Culture, there was no time to waste. It became clear very quickly the impact and role that University

Concert Hall played in the lives of not just the students and staff of UL but also of artists and audiences of all ages.

From open days to weekly lectures and student events right through to conferrings, University Concert Hall features in the journey of so many students who study at UL. The concert hall also welcomes many young aspiring dancers, musicians and singers to its stage to participate in numerous community performances, as well as young emerging artists on the cusp of their careers. There are also the many international artists and household names. From the start it was exciting to be at the helm of a venue so embedded in the university and the city.

There is another important element in concert life and that is, of course, the audience. Concerts would not be the same without our audience members, people who give life to each and every performance. From seeing the excitement of schoolchildren as they skip hand in hand through our doors for their first Christmas panto, to the anticipation of a new patron staring in awe at the *Flying Dutchman* soaring high in our atrium, or the warm friendly faces of our regular Irish Chamber Orchestra (ICO) enthusiasts – these were things we missed dearly during Covid-19 lockdowns. Online streaming had to be done. Although not the same as a live performance, it gave us a way to not just continue engaging with audiences but also to provide employment to artists and crew.

The only purpose-built concert hall in Ireland, we have had the privilege of welcoming thousands of patrons to enjoy events across the years. From classical to opera, ballet, the musicals and jazz to 'In Conversation' evenings, each one has been memorable in its own way. I have been fortunate during my time at the UCH to experience some unique concerts too. These included our twenty-fifth anniversary gala concert with the RTÉ National Symphony Orchestra led by the pipes of the late Chieftain, Paddy Moloney, who shared the stage with traditional violinist Zoë Conway and pianist Barry Douglas. One surprise guest, who got an immediate standing ovation when brought on to the orchestral sounds of 'Limerick You're A Lady', was Liam McCarthy! It was September 2018 and Liam was back in Limerick after a forty-five-year absence. We couldn't have the show without him! It was the perfect moment, capturing the essence of Limerick, culture, music, sport, pride in the city – all of which played out on our UCH stage.

Other standout evenings over the years included concerts with Limerick's own Bill Whelan and international Irish flautist Sir James Galway, 'the man with the golden flute'. Not forgetting of course Van Morrison, writer Marian Keyes and Sir Bob Geldof. Going back further, many would vividly recall shows by iconic legends at the UCH, such as Johnny Cash, Kris Kristofferson, Morrissey, Pat Shortt and Jon Kenny's record-breaking twelve-night sell-out run of *D'Unbelievables*, violinists Nigel Kennedy and Maxim Vengerov, as well as the National Youth Orchestra of Ireland's four-night Wagner *Ring Cycle*. I can't leave out *The Late Late Show* broadcast for its first trip from RTÉ's Donnybrook studios, as well as the launch and twenty-fifth anniversary celebration of RTÉ Lyric FM.

One of my more recent memorable events was the restoration of the 1932 Compton cinema pipe organ, saved from the Savoy Theatre in Cork and installed into a dedicated chamber in the concert hall on its opening in 1993, thanks to the foresight of former president Dr Ed Walsh and philanthropist Chuck Feeney. Since day one, on learning that the concert hall housed such an iconic instrument and hearing the sounds it made, I just knew the potential it had and felt that it was our responsibility as custodians to bring it back to life. After one or two failed starts, the end came in sight as I managed to secure funding from the Department of Heritage and UL. With phase one of its restoration completed, and phase two underway, I would encourage everyone to take the opportunity to attend an old Charlie Chaplin screening with organ interludes, a retro evening like no other. As the only surviving and fully intact cinema organ in Ireland, also known as the one-person orchestra, it is an experience you will not forget.

If you have had the occasion to walk through our backstage corridors, you'll have seen photographs of many visiting artists framed on our walls, a collection that continues to grow. If walls could talk, there are many intriguing stories they could share. So could many of the UCH team! It would perhaps be unwise to share the full details here. Suffice to say there were many extravagant rider requests over those years: full cooked chickens (never eaten!), rare loose-leaf tea (never drunk!), costumes designed for small dogs, and backstage parking signs developed for impresarios, producers and artists who were off the stage and on their way to Dublin before their applause finished. It is show business after all!

I consider myself fortunate to have had the opportunity to play a part in University Concert Hall's life story, and to have helped lead upgrades in recent times to enhance the experience for artists and patrons. These upgrades included a new accessible box office, pre-concert dining in Allegro, new foyer seating and a bar for patrons, as well as new lighting, sound and other technical enhancements, some of which audience members will never see but are invaluable to all visiting artists and productions.

We are lucky to have been joined on campus by a number of other arts organisations and university centres of excellence focused on the arts, from UL Orchestra to the ICO, UL Creative Writing, Sing Ireland and of course the Irish World Academy. This unique position is one that not many universities can claim and is one that continually supports and encourages artistic partnerships, planting the seeds for so many new artistic collaborations. As we face into another challenging few years, my hope is that audiences will retain the memories that were once made within our walls and that they will return to make many more.

As a Meath lady, across the last eight years I have learned many things: that hurling and rugby run in the blood of so many in the region and that University Concert Hall would not be what it is without the support of audiences, promoters, artists and patrons but also the backstage, front of house, executive team and board, who are dedicated to delivering exceptional experiences through even the toughest of times, whether the audience age is five or ninety-five. Be it through the roar of 'He's behind you', the majesty of an exceptional orchestra or hearing that legendary artist perform their most famous hit song – a live show at the UCH is what goosebumps are made of!

Sinead Hope is Director of the University Concert Hall and is a board member of Kids Classics.

CRUINNIÚ

Noel McCarthy

I started working as a porter in UL in 2005. A year later, I started the band Cruinniú (the Irish word for 'meeting'). We were originally made up of members of UL staff, but over the years this has evolved. We now include staff, UL retirees and people from the wider community in Limerick and Clare. Cruinniú holds weekly music classes, where I teach new tunes and we play selections of music we have learned over the last seventeen years.

In late 2006, after having been set up for less than six months, Cruinniú played our first public event in UL – a lunchtime concert at the Irish World Academy of Music and Dance. We had a repertoire of about thirty tunes. A sound engineer from the Irish World Academy (IWA) recorded this event and I managed to get my hands on the master tape. In conversation with the then university president, Don Barry, I outlined my wish to make a CD of our

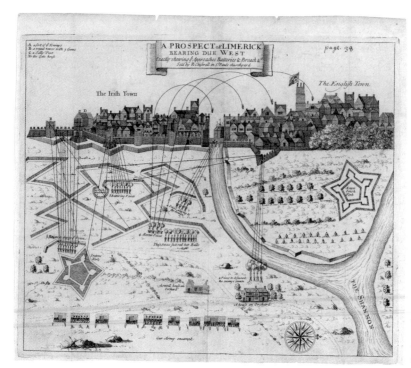

A Prospect of Limerick, Special Collections, Glucksman Library

lunchtime concert. Don agreed to sponsor it, and some months later we had raised €10,000 for St Vincent's School, Lisnagry, which caters for children between the ages of four and eighteen who have moderate general learning disabilities, severe and profound general learning disabilities, as well as autistic spectrum disorder (ASD). At the school there are four pre-school classes for children with autism from the age of three.

In 2010 we produced a DVD of music and songs in conjunction with a local primary school, Gaelscoil Chaladh an Treoigh. We titled this project *Nasc* (the Irish word for 'connection') and on it we incorporated the music of Cruinniú, with all the primary classes ag canadh amhráin i ngaeilge (singing songs in Irish). We raised over €4,000 for that school.

Cruinniú has performed at many university events, including 'Party at the Plaza'. The group has also played an active part in creating a Christmas spirit and atmosphere on campus, with our Cruinniú wrenboys performing annually in all the university restaurants over lunchtime on a set date in December.

In the 1990s I produced several music tapes promoting music and song in west Limerick, where my mother hailed from. There is a very strong wrenboy tradition in Carrigkerry in west Limerick, and I have been hunting the wren there every St Stephen's Day for nearly fifty years.

In 2006 I commenced research on the music of John McCarthy, my grand-father, whose manuscripts are housed in Special Collections at the UL Library. After six years I published a book, copies of which are available at the UL Library and the Irish Traditional Music Archive, Merrion Square, Dublin.

Today, besides continuing to teach and play music with Cruinniú, I also teach music to adults and children in Comhaltas Garraí Eoin, a Comhaltas group trying to promote our music and dance in inner-city Limerick.

Noel McCarthy is a porter in the Buildings Department at UL. He has edited the collection John McCarthy of Cappamore, Ireland: His Irish Traditional Music Manuscripts 1876–1912, Collected from the Cappamore/Silvermines area.

A DIARY OF MATESHIP AND RESILIENCE: UL ROWING CLUB

Tom McKeon

1 September 2020: Today marks the first day of the new season. I am overly eager to leave a good impression on the lads. I'm quite nervous though. I've spent the last year messing around away from rowing, trying my best to stay in shape but from the outside looking in, these guys seem like they don't mess around. I'm already off to a great start as I'm late.

26 September 2020: What a few weeks' training it has been. The group has been incredibly welcoming. I was worried it would be very serious but it's quite the opposite. Nobody is going to eat your head off for being two minutes late to training. Humans wanted, not robots. I think I've found my place in the squad. Today we had our first race of the year. It was over 3,000 metres in a single scull so it was particularly tough, but everyone in the squad outperformed themselves. Drinks with the squad tonight to celebrate! I could get used to this.

22 October 2020: The government has announced another Level Five lockdown. We're in the boathouse and the girls are overwhelmed and upset. I've never seen the lads this down either. We've packed our cars full of training equipment, ready to depart in separate directions. If we can weather this storm, I reckon we might be on to something special this season. Our home gyms consist of front rooms, utilities and sheds. Sub-prime conditions to say the least, but we're all viewing this as an opportunity.

20 November 2020: Our first fitness test of the year. I'm in the zone this morning. The warm-up goes horrendously. But my housemate, Mikey, and I have fostered an environment of stoicism over this lockdown. If an obstacle is in the way, it becomes the way. I lay down a good marker for the year and the whole squad comes out of this lockdown fitter than ever. This is just the beginning.

14 December 2020: I have just witnessed something quite extraordinary. Colm has just finished up his college exams, but he's caught up in Rowing Ireland trials at the moment and he's quite visibly banjaxed. He had a fitness test this evening and, calling a spade a spade, it was horrendous. But he stayed the course and completed the test. I reckon he could be UL's secret weapon.

4 January 2021: Another lockdown! I have a woeful feeling in my stomach that this might be a defining period in our season. I've moved back home, so unfortunately I don't have a training partner anymore. My family keep walking in when I'm training and the ventilation in the room is non-existent. Frank reminds me that to grow you have to stress the body and it will adapt. My bed now sits only a matter of metres as the crow flies from my newfound gym and some mornings it seems like a more viable option. We'll have to wait and see how this goes.

22 February 2021: I'm struggling big time. My training is suffering and I'm in a pickle mentally. I'm not motivated at all, but I don't want to let the squad down. I know I'm not the only one struggling. The support has been immense in the group chat. There is a tiny speck of light at the end of the tunnel. I wish I could support the gang more. Seeing Rory and Luke post huge sessions in this morning is keeping me going.

17 March 2021: Our final level-five lockdown fitness test. The past two-and-a-half months have taught me a lot about not only myself, but our club. My test result was nowhere near the results of the men's squad and, relatively speaking, the women's scores were streets ahead too. Lauren had an injury, yet she still managed to obtain a personal best. Corina and Ava just put their heads down and got to work. Jonny unfortunately contracted the virus, but he too pulled it out of the bag and equalled his best ever time over 2,000 metres. I keep reminding myself if it's in the way it becomes the way. I need to start believing in it again.

26 April 2021: FINALLY!! The gang is back together on the water and the craic is mighty once more. Niamh, Georgia and Finn have returned from Kerry. Mikey, Corina, Luke and Frank have left the Pale. Ava has traded the waters of Dungarvan for the Shannon. Our Mayo man, Colm, has returned from Galway (he's a blow-in Mayo 'native'). The Limerick cohort gladly make the short trip to see James Mangan standing outside the boat sheds and he welcomes us back with a soft smile. Restrictions have been lifted. We're on track … again.

19 May 2021: Our final fitness test of the year. The squad is in super shape. Our captain, Clara, had to get her wisdom teeth out, but she was adamant that she would do the 2,000-metre test before she underwent surgery. A quote from the movie *Dead Poet's Society* comes to mind as delivered by the great Robin Williams: 'Oh captain, my captain.' An inspirational figure and leader. Everyone comes out of this bout of testing with a personal best … again!

11 June 2021: A weekend off training calls for a road trip! The annual pilgrimage to Sherkin Island awaits us. 'What's the plan for the weekend?' Frank asks before we depart. A gallant James O'Donovan pipes up from the back of the boat shed: 'Shluggin'. What a gang.

17 July 2021: We are seeing the fruits of our labour. The tough programme set out by Frank, James, Ed and Brian is paying off big time. The gang are leaving the University Championships in Lough Rynn, Leitrim, with the best result UL has ever achieved. I'm watching on from my bedroom, however. I've contracted Covid-19 but my isolation ends soon. I hope to join the squad for more racing in a week's time. But for now, I'll smile at the results page, knowing that ULRC is in with a shot at the National Championships this year.

14 August 2021: We're all gathered in our separate apartments, watching the All-Ireland football semi-final. Mayo topple the favourites, Dublin. Seeing the underdogs storm away with victory, dare we dream?

20–22 August 2021: This was a weekend like no other for the university. Ten national championships. A question posed to the group during the year was: 'how many steps are there up to the podium?' Only a select few in the group could answer this at the time. Now we can all respond confidently, the answer being three. Whether you were wearing a UL T-shirt that weekend or were in one of the winning boats, everyone affiliated with the club came away from the National Rowing Centre having equally contributed to the ten victories. A rowing club once deemed 'The Graveyard' amongst those in the Irish rowing community was now top of the domestic scene. The last twelve months have proven that good teams can survive through adversity. But great organisations grow in the face of it. UL is rowing.

Tom McKeon studied Business and French at UL. At the National Rowing Championships in 2021 the UL rowers claimed ten national titles and set three new Irish records.

THE PASSENGER

Wafa Rougab

Difficult roads often lead to beautiful destinations, and life is like an ocean. It can be calm or still and rough or rigid, but in the end, it is always beautiful. To inspire people around me and leave a positive touch with every person I meet is one of my aspirations. I have always been a person who wants to make a change in the community. Therefore, I conducted a charity project in my early years of university, but there was a drive to do more. In my third year I had an 'aha moment' when I felt that I needed to make my mark in academia and that this could only be possible through research. It made me determined about pursuing my PhD.

When I was informed that my PhD would take place in Ireland, at UL specifically, I was happy that I would be a part of this great academic institution which has the reputation of being relevant to the needs of students and, hence, developing excellence in the educational field. The University of Limerick is highly recognised for its modern facilities and prides itself on being student-centred; 'Learn More', 'Live More' and 'Be More' are part of the UL ethos.

When I was provided with the necessary adaptive aids and equipment through the disability service, I felt delighted that now I would be encouraged to develop these approaches. This was possible thanks to Dr Angela Farrell, our course director, who had been in constant contact with me to guarantee getting the right equipment, always reassuring me that the disability service would provide the necessary tools. This made me realise that I didn't have to be perfect! All I had to do was adapt and enjoy the messy, imperfect and beautiful journey of my stay in Limerick. I stopped worrying about failing, and instead focused on the chances.

As a visually impaired student, I have always been the type of person who was willing to take risks and step out of my comfort zone. Studying abroad would help me realise opportunities and acquire more skills that would help develop my independence and decision-making skills for the future. Buildings and colours are a constant landmark for any place I want to localise or remember, and this increased my tie with design and architecture. As a child, I was always fascinated by beautiful buildings. Nowadays my research area is not far away from that little child's fascination. I wanted my first piece of research to reflect and represent my character, my interest and my love for arts. Therefore, I began thinking about the design of learning spaces not only from an architectural perspective but also from an educational one.

I consider myself a lucky student, as I had the chance to work with Professor Mairéad Moriarty who really made me feel comfortable and has been a strong support to me, a novice researcher. How touching and motivating words can be, especially in moments when we cease to believe in our choices. Singing on a boat during a terrible storm, we cannot stop the storm. But singing can change the hearts and spirits of the people who are together on that ship.

Little did I know that Ireland was holding other surprises. As my supervisors I was allocated Professor Helen Kelly-Holmes, a former dean of the

Arts, Humanities and Social Sciences faculty, and Professor Kerstin Mey, the first female president of a higher educational institution in Ireland. From the first meeting I had with them, I felt the warmth a researcher needs to feel with a supervisor. They were so welcoming and made sure that I got the necessary materials to help me and were very flexible in terms of offering alternative options to accommodate my visual disability. My one year under their supervision fostered my flexibility, containment and openness, and I would call my meeting with them the 'research coffee meeting' as they included me in different discussions. This inclusion increased my feeling of comfort and of self-expression, eliminating the distance that could have emerged due to their academic and administrative roles.

What makes UL special is how all the different bodies work together to ensure that students are offered not only academic advancement, but also well-being, through the counselling services and the Postgraduate Students' Union (PSU), with which I was in touch from my arrival in Ireland. The PSU worked to accommodate me in an adequate living environment, and this had a direct and positive influence on my academic achievement. Clubs and societies are also an outlet for students to practise their hobbies or be included in different activities. Indeed, everything in UL is connected through an integrated system, which would survive even the storm of the Covid-19 pandemic, which started around the time of the arrival of 132 Algerian students to UL in January 2021.

Despite these positive impressions and experiences, one cannot deny the difficulties that any international student might face, such as homesickness, and moments of loneliness and despair. However, in all these moments I had a belief that these emotions are temporary and even if they are making me feel a kind of discomfort now, experiencing them does not mean that they will last forever. Indeed, these fluctuations are a part of our nature as humans. They push us to think of ourselves as passengers on a journey into the self. This journey might have an ending date, but it will live with me for the rest of my life, because I am now a thousand miles away from the version that I used to be a year ago;

now a version that survived ups and downs, that keeps whispering nice songs, reminding me of the joyful moments, moments of sadness, and the beautiful people who are a remedy for the pain and a lighthouse to guide us when the waves are very high. These people are a strong, magical asset that will remain in my heart and life forever. Thus, Ireland will be a country of renaissance for me, and for all of us, at so many different levels. I am waiting with open arms for the beautiful things and experiences that it still has to offer.

Wafa Rougab, from Laghouat Algeria, has a Master's degree in Literature and Civilization. In January 2021 she became a PhD student at UL.

FORGIVENESS NOT PERMISSION: TEACHING DESIGN AT UL

Muireann McMahon

For several months during the first graduating year of Product Design in 2007, a coffin occupied space in the design studio. A student, whose family owned an undertaking business, was designing a method of moving coffins around the funeral home and he needed the coffin to build and test prototypes. We got so blasé about the coffin being there that we would lean on it while chatting and rest our coffee cups on it during project reviews.

But having a coffin in the studio wasn't as easy an experience for everyone. Some people found its presence triggering and uncomfortable. Not for the first time, it struck me that products have significance in the meaning we attach to them, the emotions they evoke and the unique experience of every person across that product's life story. The experience of the coffin also reinforced the realisation that working in the design studio was never going to be boring.

Not many people understand what product designers do, despite being surrounded by their work in our everyday lives; from the mundane objects to the life-transforming. I have always had an interest in design, from when I was a child making transport modes (cars and hot air balloons) from shoeboxes for my Barbies. But I had never planned on becoming a design educator, nor had I intended coming back to Limerick even though it is where I was born and raised. I had thought I was going to be a famous designer taking my place amongst the other design legends like Philippe Starck, Henry Dreyfuss and Eileen Gray, but in the third year of my own degree, I realised this wasn't going to be the case. I honestly didn't know what specific area of product design I was interested in or what impact I wanted to create through my work. Studying Industrial Design, first at UL and then at the National College of Art and Design, had given me such a broad base of skills that I couldn't choose, or maybe didn't want to. After messing around in the commercial furniture and interiors realm and contemplating several options for further education, including one in funfair design, I applied for and got a job as an Assistant Lecturer in IT Carlow. Both my parents were teachers, so I imagine that a move into education was inevitable.

During my time at UL, I've seen many projects undertaken and products and systems developed. Some have been more successful than others, but it isn't always the most ground-breaking ones, those that won prizes or made it to market, that leave lasting memories. What remains with me are the projects that were fun, dangerous, joyful, or frustrating; the projects that challenged me and the other tutors. Often, these were projects that come from the designer's personal and family's story, like the face mask and testing system we worked on in 2018, designed for immunocompromised people, to enable participation in social gatherings. If we had only known then what we know now.

Other great projects included the breathing device for bed-bound patients, the diving equipment, the menstrual cup, the breast drain, the cardiac surgical

device, the flatpack home office, the suite of devices for young adults with ASD, the conservation beehive, the shelter system for rough sleepers. The list goes on.

The annual 'Product, Design and Technology (guerrilla) Go-kart Race' was a classic example of a project that was pure fun (albeit a bit dangerous). My abiding memory is of a student careening down the hill in a self-designed, self-made go-kart. They belted towards the Rowing Club in a hamster wheel that had to fit into two Ryanair overhead luggage bags and be assembled just before the race began. Since then, speed bumps have been installed on that particular road and, while the two may not be connected, needless to say, permission was not sought from Buildings and Estates. (Sorry!) We have a saying among the design staff: 'Ask for forgiveness, not permission.' The aim is to do what needs to be done so the students can create work of value and impact, that they have the freedom to try things and, most importantly, make mistakes in the doing. Learning to build something that functions, to play with material properties, to calculate mechanical movements, to test your design with the class and celebrate victory or even just finishing the PDT Go-kart Race unscathed, is a highlight for our graduates.

We're very lucky that we have the design studio, which offers a space for people to be creative, to connect, innovate and be excited about the potential of design. But design is a messy business as it involves making, building, testing, sticking stuff together (also to tables and to each other), dismantling the chairs and cutting the desks (to the cleaning staff for dealing with our mess: sorry and thank you!). There is a lot of working through ideas to tease out details, to refine form, function and user experience. I remember a student sitting outside my office window wearing a prototype for a climbing helmet while his class-mate stood on the roof two floors up dropping stones on his head. (Needless to say, Health and Safety were not consulted. Sorry! Please note we are now fully compliant with all Health and Safety and Buildings guidelines.) He was testing durability, fit and material choice for the helmet, so it all made sense in the end. From the perceived chaos, great ideas emerge. It's the surprise and relief when everything comes together that makes all the effort worthwhile. When the paint dries on a prototype, when the sketches are stuck on the wall, when the graphics are printed and mounted, the creativity and innovation become tangible.

Even in the moments when I am tearing my hair out, the projects, the students and my colleagues in the design studio excite me, keeping me curious, engaged, exploring and constantly questioning. Now, as we move into an era where our resources become scarcer, our habits come under sharper scrutiny and our choices need to become more considered and considerate, design asks us to think deeply about our consumption habits, the value we place on products, the stories we attach, the care we take of them and the footprint they leave.

Dr Muireann McMahon lectures on the BSc Product Design and Technology, UL School of Design. After her PhD from Loughborough Design School, 2013, she was Scholar in Residence with Designmatters Art Center, California.

SANC·TU·ARY | \ 'SAŊ(K)-CHƎ-,WER-Ē: A PLACE WHERE SOMEONE OR SOMETHING IS PROTECTED OR GIVEN SHELTER

John Lannon

Reimagining the living library of knowledge that sits on the banks of the Shannon as a place of sanctuary is easy when we try. In amongst the economics, engineering, equine science and English, there is a door that provides access to education for people pushed to the margins of society. Members of one group in particular, people with or applying for refugee status, have come through that door. It was pushed open by a small cohort within the campus community. And when it was ajar, others widened the gap so that the international on our doorstep became part of our classrooms.

The official designation of University of Sanctuary came in 2017, and by 2021 there were graduates that had worked their way through degree programmes.

There are financial, administrative and institutional barriers that condemn thousands of young and eager asylum seekers to years of idleness in Ireland. But providing what were called Sanctuary scholarships was a pathway in from the margins for some new arrivals in Ireland. It was, as one student put it, an opportunity to progress in life, rather than 'stagnating in the bleak provision of a DP [Direct Provision] centre'.

The life story of a young man who fled oppression in Afghanistan comes to mind. He undertook the Mature Student Access Certificate course, progressed to a degree programme, took time out to cope with the traumatic experiences with which life had presented him, returned and progressed.

Progression is a word we use a lot in the world of academia. Demonstrating that one's ability and effort can be combined into something worthy of survival in the academic system is a measure of success. But for someone who has fled a life-threatening situation, made a perilous journey across two continents and then waited five years for the Irish government to give him protection, its meaning cannot be compared to what a twenty-year-old from Ireland's mid-west imagines. Yet the essence of an institution that offers sanctuary is that everyone's progress is recognised and celebrated. We just need different ways to do our recognising and celebrating.

The University of Sanctuary Ireland initiative was set up to encourage and celebrate the good practice of universities, colleges and other education institutes across Ireland in welcoming refugees, asylum seekers and other migrants into their communities. Fostering a culture of welcome and inclusion for people seeking sanctuary sat well with UL's support for access and participation of students from groups under-represented in the third-level sector. The university responded to the call in 2017 by inviting international protection applicants who were living in Direct Provision to enrol for access and degree programmes. The response was positive. Applicants enrolled, and the campus community learned a little about what it was like to be a refugee.

And yet, there was something missing.

I remember a day in July 2018 when an exhibition entitled 'War-Torn

Children' was opened in the Central Buildings Gallery in Limerick's O'Connell Street. It was an exhibition of arpilleras that highlighted the devastating impact of war on children, their families and communities. Arpilleras are brightly coloured patchwork pictures and they were originally made by women (arpilleristas) who had been left in a state of financial insecurity due to widespread unemployment and forced disappearances of their husbands and children in Chile. They were made primarily from scraps of cloth and depicted political themes through scenes of impoverished living conditions and government repression. Through the arpilleras in the War-Torn Children exhibition we saw the world through the eyes and artistic expression of people who knew about oppression. There was an expression of history and resistance that those of us who do not bear witness are privileged to see.

The voices of people with lived experience of the exclusion and oppression we see on our screens are central to our learning. So, too, is the opportunity to listen to women and men who speak truth to power. That missing piece, the voices of articulate, emotive survivors, witnesses, commentators and allies, is now emerging in UL. It's in the classrooms, the social enterprises, the research labs, the online conversations. It's in the response of the journal *Unapologetic* to the social issues of contemporary Ireland. It's in the *Gorm Media* curation of common ground through conversations. And it's where equality, diversity and inclusion become real.

A university needs to be a living place that reflects the struggles and the grief and the joys that humanity experiences. It needs to be a collective that bears witness, deepens our understanding, and plants the seeds of a sustainable future in the worlds of business, politics, sport and more. But it must also be a place where everyone feels safe. And protected. The fact that there are eighty-two million refugees in the world today is a social, political and environmental problem of extraordinary proportions. But for every refugee that arrives in Limerick there is a unique personal crisis that our humanity requires us to respond to.

My own journey has taken me through a variety of UL doors, starting in 1984 when I was based in the Electronics Department for a few short months. Most recently I've been privileged to be able to take the short journey from UL into town, to help the local migrant and refugee rights organisation Doras to advocate for the changes that are needed. The university is a vital source of sustenance for the organisation, providing volunteers, research partnerships, and willing co-conspirators in our fight against injustice. As such, it is embodying the three principles that underpin being a University of Sanctuary. These are learning, welcoming and sharing. Learning involves developing an understanding of the global and local dynamics that force people to move, and their subsequent experiences. Welcoming means actively including people who are asylum seekers or refugees in the campus community and making them welcome. And sharing is about imparting what has been learned with other education institutions, the local community and others.

Education is a key that opens doors, creates opportunities, and builds a

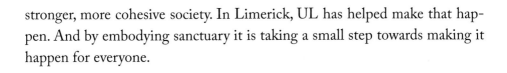

stronger, more cohesive society. In Limerick, UL has helped make that happen. And by embodying sanctuary it is taking a small step towards making it happen for everyone.

John Lannon is CEO of Doras, a Limerick–based migrant support and human rights organisation. He is currently on a career break from UL's Kemmy Business School.

REFLECTIONS FROM A WORK AND ORGANISATIONAL PSYCHOLOGIST: FROM THEORY TO INTERVENTION

Deirdre O'Shea

Psychologists love theories. We theorise about why people behave in particular ways, what motivates their behaviours and why their behaviour changes when they are in groups or alone. Like any psychologist, I love a good theory. I chose to study an applied area of psychology which focuses on the practical application of these theories in order to help employees and organisations be more productive and stay healthy in the workplace.

In terms of its academic home, Work and Organisational Psychology varies as to whether it is located in psychology departments or business schools across universities. From the time I studied for my Master's and PhD, I have been located in a business school, which continued when I joined the Kemmy

Business School at the University of Limerick in 2008. This has been useful in tempering my natural tendency to admire a nice, shiny theory for its own sake, and has kept me focused on how knowledge of psychology can help to solve issues of performance and well-being in work settings. That said, you can't take the theory out of a psychologist. My approach to developing a solution to any work-related issue always starts with a good theory.

Early research in work and organisational psychology tended to focus on the role of traits and abilities, how they were linked to performance, and how we could assess cognitive abilities and personality to select the right person for the right job. Although these are still important research and applied topics in Work and Organisational Psychology, personality in particular is really only so-so in terms of being able to predict specific behaviours. Besides that, in my experience, there is a tendency to misinterpret personality assessments as deterministic in some way, when in fact it is quite the opposite, reflecting merely one's preferred behaviours in the absence of any stronger contextual signals for how one should behave. It does seem, though, that one of my preferred behaviours (or traits, call it what you will) is 'being organised' (or that's what others tell me), which may explain why I gravitated to the topic of self-regulation when I began my research career. Self-regulation represents a set of skills and processes which can be learned and developed. It looks at the processes and strategies through which we manage our thoughts, emotions, motivation and behaviour,[1] reflecting volitional and effortful acts. It has been said that self-regulation is one of the best hopes for psychology to make a broad, positive contribution to human welfare, and is amenable to change.[2] What's not to like!? In addition to the fit between my proclivity for organisation and the topic of self-regulation, it is an area replete with lots and lots of fairly complicated theories!

As I came to the end of my PhD in 2011, I had done some nice theorising about self-regulation and some research that I, at least, thought was interesting. However, I was still struggling with how to utilise this to good effect. The missing piece of the puzzle came about when I met four other like-minded researchers at the European Association of Work and Organisational Psychology Early

Career Summer School in Gandia in Spain. By the end of the week, we had crafted a project to investigate whether the proliferation of positive psychology interventions in workplace situations was warranted. At the time, positive psychology was on the crest of a wave, and its inherent attractiveness (who doesn't want to focus on the positive in life?!) meant that these types of activities were being offered to employees, with little consideration of whether they were appropriate or effective. This prompted a research collaboration which has lasted over a decade and won us a best paper award in 2019 for our research,[3] as well as research funding successes. Over this time, we have pushed the field forward, demonstrating that certain types of positive psychology activities can indeed have some effects – but they tend to be small – and that a key factor determining whether they are effective for a given person in a given situation is to understand the psychological mechanisms through which they work, as well as the individual and contextual boundary conditions. These often boil down to some kind of resources, whether psychological or situational, and so, we quickly pivoted our focus to the investigation of resource-based interventions in work settings,[4] organising a small conference in Heidelberg, Germany on this topic is 2013, and publishing a special issue in *Journal of Occupational and Organisational Psychology* in 2015.

We have investigated a number of resource-based/positive psychology interventions for use in workplace settings, and much to my joy, many of these activities are founded in self-regulation. We have focused on the effectiveness of these interventions when used on a daily basis (in keeping with the trend away from the study of static traits towards more dynamic approaches of the day-to-day experience of workers) and whether utilising such daily micro-interventions can build over time. One such intervention is mindfulness, which refers to an attitude of being aware of and attentive to one's momentary thoughts and emotions, in a non-judgemental way.[5] It consists of regulating the focus of one's attention and approaching situations and experiences with an attitude of openness and non-judgement.[6] Practising mindfulness can increase daily positive emotions and decrease daily negative emotions.[7] It can also be used to aid workers to separate their work and home life (as a cognitive-emotional segmentation strategy) which can help employees to detach from work at the end of the workday.[8] Mindfulness can thus develop skills to enhance the experience of work for individuals, but should not be used as a replacement for managing workloads and designing meaningful jobs.[9]

Positive reflection or recalling positive work events can help employees to focus on positive thoughts about their work, rather than ruminating about it.[10] Our research has found that engaging in positive thinking, particularly when the positive meaning of one's work is emphasised in the activity, has more significant benefits for workers who have a higher need for recovery (a sign of impaired work-related well-being),[11] reducing emotional exhaustion and chronic fatigue and promoting experiences of hope and optimism.[12] Positive reappraisal interventions go further than positive reflection and train individuals to reframe thoughts and situations to think about events in a more positive or beneficial way.[13] Our research has demonstrated positive reappraisal can decrease the level of negative emotions an individual experiences on a daily basis.[14] In addition, we have found that pairing positive reappraisal with mindfulness can lead to more immediate effects in terms of changing daily positive and negative emotions.[15]

In contrast, savouring nature is a less cognitively taxing intervention, which uses an emotion regulation strategy of savouring to enhance the attentional draw of nature. Engaging in such activities can restore our daily zest or vigour for work.[16] This also points to some of the boundary conditions for the effectiveness of micro-interventions. For example, we found some evidence to suggest positive reflection, positive reappraisal and mindfulness take effort to engage in, and that individuals need to have a reason to utilise them, whether that be personal (such as low need for recovery)[17] or interpersonal.[18]

Overall, our research suggests that there is no 'one size fits all' intervention. Positive psychology and resource-based interventions can have benefits for the individual, but predominantly should be seen as ways to develop certain self-regulation or emotion-regulation skills which can maintain psychological resources that help individuals to better manage their experience of work and stress. However, we need to do more to ensure there is a fit between the intervention activity and the needs of the individual. Whether they are appropriate depends both on the individual and the workplace or work situation. Like any skill, these activities need to be practised regularly and there is likely benefit to practising a variety of approaches. Finally, such interventions should not be offered as a solution to employee well-being, particularly when organisational level or job level changes are necessary.

Notes

1   O'Shea, D., F. Buckley, and J. Halbesleben, 'Self-regulation in entrepreneurs: Integrating action, cognition, motivation, and emotions', *Organizational Psychology Review*, 7(3) (2017), pp. 250–78.

2   Forgas, J.P., R.F. Baumeister, and D.M. Tice, *The Psychology of Self-Regulation: An Introductory Review*, in idem (eds), *Psychology of Self-Regulation: Cognitive, Affective and Motivational Processes* (Psychology Press, 2009), pp. 1–20.

3   Steidle, A., et al., 'Energizing respites from work: a randomized controlled study on respite interventions', *European Journal of Work and Organizational Psychology*, 26(5) (2017), pp. 650–62.

4   Michel, A., D. O'Shea, and A. Hoppe, 'Designing and evaluating resource-oriented interventions to enhance employee well-being and health', *Journal of Occupational and Organizational Psychology*, 88(3) (2015), pp. 459–63.

5   Baer, R.A., 'Mindfulness training as a clinical intervention: A conceptual and empirical review', *Clinical Psychology-Science and Practice*, 10(2) (2003), pp. 125–43.

6   Bishop, S.R., et al., 'Mindfulness: A proposed operational definition', *Clinical Psychology-Science and Practice*, 11(3) (2004), pp. 230–41.

7   Pogrebtsova, E., et al., 'Exploring daily affective changes in university students with a mindful positive reappraisal intervention: A daily diary randomized controlled trial', *Stress and Health*, 34(1) (2018), pp. 46–58.

8   Michel, A., C. Bosch, and M. Rexroth, 'Mindfulness as a cognitive-emotional segmentation strategy: An intervention promoting work-life balance', *Journal of Occupational and Organizational Psychology*, 87(4) (2014), pp. 733–54.

9   O'Shea, D., et al., 'Positive psychology interventions and employee wellbeing: When and for whom are they effective?', in A. Kinder, R. Hughes, and C. Cooper (eds), *Occupational Health and Well-Being* (Routledge, forthcoming).

10 Ibid.

11 Sonnentag, S. and F.R.H. Zijlstra, 'Job characteristics and off-job activities as predictors of need for recovery, well-being, and fatigue', *Journal of Applied Psychology*, 91(2) (2006), pp. 330–50.

12 Clauss, E., et al., 'Promoting Personal Resources and Reducing Exhaustion Through Positive Work Reflection Among Caregivers', *Journal of Occupational Health Psychology*, 23(1) (2018), pp. 127–40.

13 Gross, J.J., 'Antecedent- and response-focused emotion regulation: Divergent consequences for experience, expression, and physiology', *Journal of Personality and Social Psychology*, 74(1) (1998), pp. 224–37.

14 Pogrebtsova, E., et al., 'Exploring daily affective changes'.

15 Ibid.

16 Steidle, A., et al., 'Energizing respites from work'.

17 Clauss, E., et al., 'Promoting Personal Resources and Reducing Exhaustion'.

18 Molina, A. and D. O'Shea, 'Mindful Emotion Regulation, Savouring and Proactive Behaviour: The Role of Supervisor Justice', *Applied Psychology: An International Review – Psychologie Appliquee : Revue Internationale*, 69(1) (2020), pp. 148–75.

Deirdre O'Shea is Senior Lecturer in Work and Organisational Psychology at the Kemmy Business School, UL. Her research interests include psychological resource-based interventions, self-regulation, and emotion regulation.

COMPOSING WITH COMPUTERS

Mikael Fernström

*I may not have gone where I intended to go, but I think I have
ended up where I needed to be.*

Douglas Adams, *The Long Dark Tea-Time of the Soul*

In the early 1990s UL was a techie place. I always found science and technology fascinating. I was working freelance at the time, based in Plassey
Technological Park. In 1995 Liam Bannon, who had recently joined UL,
sent around a survey to businesses in the Tech Park, to which I responded.
Following this, Liam contacted me for a chat that eventually developed into
his suggestion that I 'should hang around for a while'. Which I did for twenty-
five years.

Little did he or anybody else at UL know that, while science and technology
dominated my résumé, those were only half of my interests and skills. The other

half is in art, in particular sound and music. Over the years my surroundings at UL gradually discovered this duality of mine.

Together with a couple of postgrads and, sometimes, visiting researchers, my first years at UL were spent in the Foundation Building. We mere mortals were in the open plan office space, while faculty resided in the surrounding offices. As it happened, Liam Bannon's and Mícheál Ó Súilleabháin's groups were neighbours. This often led to interesting exchanges of ideas. My work was research on sonic browsing. It was exciting to explore selective hearing when the whole open office landscape was sometimes bursting with conversations and other sounds, sometimes music.

In 1997 I outlined a vision of an interactive dance floor with the possibility for our neighbour researchers to gather data about Irish dancing. We were given a small budget to build what was to be called the LiteFoot interactive dance floor, which was premiered in Mícheál Ó Súilleabháin's Toyota concert in the University Concert Hall, with Catherine Foley doing a short Irish dance performance, demonstrating some of the possibilities of LiteFoot. Following this, Catherine and the LiteFoot were featured on RTÉ's *The Late Late Show*. The demo concept at the time was quite simple, coloured blobs on screen and synthesised musical sounds in a pentatonic scale, all controlled by the dancer in real time.

In 1998 I organised a workshop, 'Performing Arts Electrocuted', with invited speakers Joe Paradiso, Todd Winkler, Phil Ellis and Antonio Camurri. I was hoping that this could serve as inspiration for a UL Master's programmes in Music Technology and Interactive Media. After the workshop, one of the participants, Sean Taylor from the Limerick School of Art and Design, approached me and asked if it was possible to make music from weather maps. He had been cutting out the daily weather map from *The Irish Times* for several months; flicking through the pieces of newspaper worked as an animation. I tried to explain how I would do this, which became the start of a collaboration lasting more than twenty years, that we named Softday. Our first project 'Bliain Le Baisteach' (A Year of Rainfall) was selected to be part of Ireland's pavilion at

the millennium World Expo in Hannover and the project received funding to get the ICO to perform the work. The ICO had become orchestra-in-residence at UL in 1995. Hearing my music performed live by the ICO in the University Concert Hall is still, to this day, one of my life highlights.

The event was also the reason for another experiment: to do live video streaming of the performance in the UCH via the web. At that time, there was no network or server capability on HEAnet that could facilitate thousands of simultaneous video streams. Through an informal collaboration with a European telecom company, we used four ISDN lines (normally used for point-to-point video conferencing at UL) to connect to servers in Stockholm from where a number of servers delivered video. It was an interesting experiment and it worked.

It was a good time to be working in computer science at UL. The Master's programmes in Music Technology and in Interactive Media meant that technical and physical resources for music and media production became available. For several years around the millennium and onwards, Donncha Ó Maidín was head of computer science, which helped facilitate the department in terms of music technology resources. He also shared an interest in the digital representation of music, with all its beautiful complexities. For me as a composer and creative media person it was an excellent place to be.

There used to be an anechoic chamber at UL, a small room with very peculiar acoustics: there was no noticeable reverberation. This was apparently a leftover from the UL physics department. It was a great little resource for exploring listening and possibilities for virtual acoustics. It was in this kind of room that the American composer John Cage claimed to have heard his own nervous system and blood flow, as well as getting inspired for his famous work *4'33"*. Unfortunately, UL demolished its anechoic chamber in 2005, as the School of Architecture needed space. It wasn't until 2008, when a colleague called Kerry Hagan headed up an initiative to set up the Spatialization and Auditory Display Environment (SpADE), that we could resume virtual acoustics research, and in 2010 SpADE was given a semi-permanent home in a large room in the basement of the Glucksman Library.

One of the main themes in my research is to augment, not replace, human ability by means of computing. I had started to write musical algorithms (creating rules, calculations and problem-solving) in the 1980s, long before joining UL. During my time at UL, I had ample opportunities to continue this work and bring it to audiences. In hindsight, it is nice to feel that I found myself in the right place at the right time.

Mikael Fernström, former Director of the Interaction Design Centre, taught at UL's Department of Computer Science and Information Systems from 1996 to 2020. He now works independently, based in West Cork.

AN IRISH-GERMAN PERSPECTIVE ON UL@50 – OR CIGS@25

Gisela Holfter

U L@50 in 2022/23. Not a bad year for the fiftieth anniversary, as it means the institution has a great year ahead for its 250th anniversary: 2222!

I wonder what UL will look like then. Two hundred years ahead is difficult to imagine, as so much can happen in that timespan. Two hundred years ago there was only one university in Ireland. However, even a span of fifty years of institutional history is too long for me to reflect upon with any meaningful personal insights. When UL started, I had not yet begun primary school. So it's just as well that I will focus on another anniversary: twenty-five years of the Centre for Irish-German Studies at UL, founded in 1997. I believe the way it started and has developed since might also say something about the university.

With the enthusiasm of someone who was in her first year of a permanent position and just back from a conference in Riga where I was invited to open an exhibition on the German writer Heinrich Böll, I said to my colleague Joachim Fischer that it would be great to organise a conference on Irish-German relations. Joachim, who like me had chosen the area for his PhD, was taken by the idea. He had even thought of a research centre in the area. I said something along the lines of, 'Okay, let's do it'. And we did.

In September 1997 we organised the inaugural conference, focusing on the history, literature and translation of Böll (who had received the Nobel Prize in Literature twenty-five years before) and his *Irisches Tagebuch*, published forty years previously. There have been seventeen international conferences since. More are planned, and there have been many smaller colloquia, lectures, readings, concerts and exhibitions, research projects, publications, including an Irish-German Studies book series, Irish Research Council fellowship, scholarships and many other grants. Our aims are still the same: the centre is to encourage and facilitate interdisciplinary research into all aspects of contacts between Ireland and the German-speaking countries; to create a forum of discussion for interested parties, in the form of seminars, guest lectures and conferences; to co-ordinate and encourage the compilation of Irish material on Austria, Germany and Switzerland and German-language material on Ireland as a resource base for researchers; and to increase knowledge about German-speaking countries, their societies and cultures, as well as Irish-German relations in the region, and further promote mutual understanding. The building up of a book collection was greatly enhanced by the donation of the Gottschalk Collection, the largest private collection of German material on Ireland, by the late Jürgen Gottschalk, the founder of the Würzburg Irish-German Society, and by other donations. We have grown from two members to almost thirty, both in UL and Mary Immaculate College and further afield in Ireland, Germany, the United Kingdom and Italy.

Letting two assistant lecturers start off a new research centre is something that older universities probably wouldn't have allowed. More likely than not, it would have been the prerogative of the chair of the discipline. We never had a chair in German (or Irish for that matter). On the one hand, one could argue that this opened up initiatives such as ours, but on the other hand the lack of professorial positions in Modern Languages (the chair in French was phased out when the last incumbent retired) has also contributed to a reduced visibility within the university and outside, despite the excellent work done by colleagues in the School of Modern Languages and Applied Linguistics.

It has not always been plain sailing, there were low points as well. I recall a time when there was an attempt to close the centre as there was a feeling that there should be more critical mass (colleagues at other universities didn't seem to count at that particular point). In fairness, it wasn't just us being singled out, other smaller centres were also threatened. No action was taken and we simply went on, maybe actually more determined. And throughout the last twenty-five years we did have support for our events from each and every UL president.

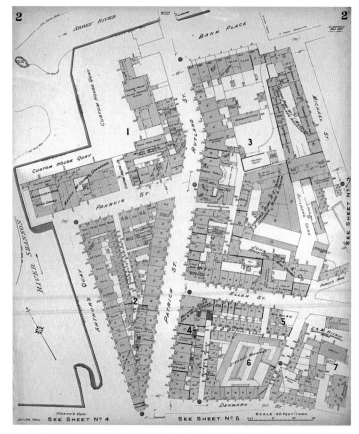

Goad Insurance Map, Special Collections, Glucksman Library

They opened our international conferences and continuously indicated to visiting ambassadors and other VIPs that the work we do was seen as worthwhile. Likewise, we have had support from our deans and heads of school.

One of the highlights happened in 2021 when the centre was instrumental in attracting German President Frank-Walter Steinmeier to UL during his state visit to Ireland. He and his Irish counterpart, Michael D. Higgins, spent some time perusing some of the jewels of the Gottschalk Collection among other treasures of the Special Collections in the Glucksman Library. Our proposal to include UL and Limerick in the state visit of the German president received the backing of the German ambassador and the Irish ambassador and led to a visit of the protocol team from both the German and the Irish side, vetting all potential venues. The offerings of the book collection and UL were sufficiently convincing. Quite often UL, its campus and facilities still seem to be a well-kept secret, but they tend to hugely impress unsuspecting visitors. This was brought home to me in the context of the same state visit, at the dinner hosted by President Steinmeier, when my table neighbour turned out to be the foreign affairs adviser to the German president. After hearing my background, he said, 'Yes, I understand we will be going there tomorrow,' with a rather questioning expression, as if he couldn't quite understand why. It was extremely gratifying when another diner at the table joined the conversation at that stage and informed the adviser that he had a treat in store. The diner was a former Irish ambassador to Germany who had been at the Irish-German diplomatic gathering (with seven current and former diplomats and the Secretary General of the Department of Foreign Affairs) we had organised in 2019 in the context of ninety years of Irish-German diplomatic relations (which led Frank McNally to muse in *The Irish Times*: 'What might the collective term for a gathering of diplomats be? A whisper? A (garden) party? A bag? I can't decide, but whatever you call it, there will be one in the University of Limerick today.'). The former Irish ambassador to Germany continued to say that he had to admit he had never been to UL before but was 'blown away'.

I am still blown away by UL quite frequently, after almost twenty-eight years here myself, and I consider myself lucky on so many fronts. A most beautiful campus, really wonderful colleagues and students who engage with and sometimes get hooked on Irish-German topics. Here is to twenty-five, fifty, no, 200 more years of Irish-German Studies at the University of Limerick!

Associate Professor Gisela Holfter is Director of the Centre for Irish–German Studies at UL. Her research interests include Irish–German cultural and historical relations, German literature and exile studies.

TWO TRAINS OF THOUGHT

Bill Whelan

I n 1971 members of the Irish Women's Liberation Movement boarded the train from Dublin to Belfast with a hoard of contraceptives. Arriving back in Connolly Station, they engaged in a well-publicised challenge to the authorities and the outmoded laws against family planning. Their actions ultimately led to the Family Planning Act when contraception was legalised.

Some five years previously, in April 1966, hundreds of pupils from the schools of Limerick, Clare and Tipperary boarded a specially booked train to Dublin under the banner of the LSUPC (Limerick Students' University Project Committee). I was fifteen at the time and I recall the excitement as we assembled at 'The Railway', or Colbert Station as it is now known, for a very noisy train ride.

On arrival we paraded through the streets of Dublin led by the CBS Pipe Band and finally down Marlborough Street to the Department of Education, while a delegation from the student group met with the then Minister for Education, George Colley, as well as our own Donogh O'Malley, a Limerick man. As the discussions went on inside the department, we crowded outside in an unseasonably cold April and sang what had become the anthem of the movement – Woody Guthrie's 'This Land is Your Land'.

> This land is your land, this land is my land,
> From California to the New York island,
> From the redwood forest to the Gulf Stream waters,
> This land was made for you and me.

Although this song first appeared in the 1940s, it was revived by many folk artists in the 1950s and 1960s, including Peter, Paul and Mary, and The Seekers. Its lyrics had little to do with the aspirations of a group of freezing schoolchildren pleading for a University for Limerick, but that didn't matter. It was the spirit that counted, and this song roundly raised the spirits.

An elderly Jesuit who taught us in the Crescent used to say, while waving a cautionary finger, 'Gentlemen, you are living in stirring times.' Bob Dylan had predicted it when he wrote 'The Times They Are a-Changin'', which The Byrds took on to further chart success in 1966. The Vietnam War was in full swing and there was a heady whiff in the air that a new generation was about to make some very strong cultural and political statements that would turn the old world on its axis. We had already witnessed the assassination of John F. Kennedy and would later see Martin Luther King and Robert Kennedy felled, with their dreams shattered beside them.

These early seismic shudderings were being felt everywhere. Limerick was no exception. There was a lively music scene in the city, and various groups like Reform and Grannies Intentions were giving voice to an emerging counter-culture as the 'beat groups' began to unseat the showbands. On the international scene we were not just hearing the voices of protest like Dylan, Donovan and Barry Maguire with his 'Eve of Destruction' but were also being exposed to the sparkling inventiveness of The Beatles and The Beach Boys, as well as the Dadaist lunacy of Frank Zappa and the Mothers of Invention. All bets were off. The pop charts, if nothing else a measure of the preoccupations of the young, were a broad church where you could find The Bachelors nestled up beside The Who, and Ken Dodd rubbing shoulders with Aretha Franklin.

It is hardly a surprise that in this turbulent multiverse, the young people of Limerick became impatient for a third-level institution. We were a city – the *urbs antiqua* – and the least we deserved was an institution of learning to educate our youth and to match the others on this island. So the LSUPC was formed from the embers of an earlier university project. Under the guidance of Gerry O'Malley and an energetic committee, our government and media were showered with an insistent letter-writing campaign and a series of public demonstrations, fund raisers and marches.

And so on that April morning, hundreds of us heard the call, donned our scarves and overcoats, made flasks of tea and ham sandwiches, unfurled our banners and marched on Dublin.

The night before we left, a few of us put on an album by The Impressions and listened to Curtis Mayfield sing these lyrics.

> People get ready, there's a train a-comin'
> Don't need no baggage, you just get on board,
> All you need is faith to hear that diesel hummin'
> Don't need no ticket, you just thank the Lord.

And we didn't need a ticket, thanks to the LSUPC.

In 1968 I left Limerick and began my studies at UCD. In those days the university was in Earlsfort Terrace, and with Trinity College down the road, the inner city teemed with student life. In later years, when I moved to Connemara, I saw how the university in Galway contributes so much to the life of that city, as indeed, UCC does in Cork. I am occasionally surprised when students tell me that they rarely go into Limerick.

My hope for UL is for a more intimate and meaningful integration with the city from which it gets its name.

Today, as I sit and listen or perform in the University Concert Hall or hear young musicians at the Irish World Academy of Music and Dance, or wander around this very impressive campus, I remember those days in the 1960s when we dreamed. Not all of the promises of the 1960s became realities – but this one certainly did.

Grammy winner Bill Whelan is a celebrated composer who has worked with U2 and Kate Bush, among many others. His iconic music for Riverdance *is loved all over the world.*

BLUEBELLS

Clodagh O'Gorman

I have always been enchanted by them. Strong and slender, blue and green, not to be seen together on an Irish *cailín*. But they can carry these colours, these belles in blue. They bend, sway, dance, twinkle, each movement like a note of music, singing, chiming. They bend, but they don't break. Maybe if someone stands upon them. But not often. A friendly little flower, growing in small clusters, surrounded by like-spirited dancing blue bells, a chorus of twinkling dancers. Nearby, another cluster. Over there, another.

They have captivated me since I was a child. A nearby garden, not mine, behind a tall grey stone wall. A secret door to my secret garden. They were not for a vase; bluebells don't dance in a vase. I could only watch them, listen to them, see them, hear them. Every year, without fail, as reliable as the waves beating relentlessly on the beach, they grew under that old beech tree, crops

and choruses, dancing not breaking, twinkling and chiming.

So, when I had children of my own, I hoped for our own secret garden of bluebells. Bluebells that might twinkle and dance across the generations. I spent a (relatively) ridiculous amount of money on bluebell bulbs. They were brown, not blue. I had hoped for blue bulb bells. We planted them. Hands hurt from digging the cold, hard ground on an unforgiving winter's evening. Under the beech tree, bare now, naked of its glorious autumn leaf dress.

And we waited for the familiar and glorious sea of blue to appear. Nothing. Not a thing. Not a bluebell to be seen, not a bluebell to be heard. The grand beech tree redressed and undressed, redressed and undressed, redressed and undressed, but never did it wear its bluebell shoes.

Three long years we waited. I had almost given up all hope. And then, they appeared. Magically. Overnight. The most glorious and tiny crop of bluebells we had ever seen. They were tiny, but strong. They bent, swayed, danced twinkled in their daring blue glow. They sang to us. And we danced and sang with joy that the bluebells had grown. And the following year, another crop over there.

Now we rely on them every year, the appearance of the bluebells, the glorious blue and green, the beech tree redressing from the ground up, its little army of bluebells announcing the arrival of a new year, a good year, a bluebell year. As steady and relentless as the waves. Ready to enchant again, another dance, another twinkle, another song, another child.

Clodagh O'Gorman is the Foundation Chair of Paediatrics at UL School of Medicine and Consultant Paediatrician at University Hospital Limerick.

ORDNANCE SURVEY, 1974

Eoin Devereux

With neither map nor compass,
Ordnance House, Newtown Mahon
is my starting point,
as I traipse the street
of the mad,
the dead,
and the bad.

At the pitch-pine gates of Shaw's bloody slaughterhouse,
the sweet and sour smell of pig-shit wafts over the squeals
of terror,
the siren beckons clogged pork butchers,

sharpening their knives of steel,
to carve the finest cuts of ham and bacon,
for the bone china plates of the well-heeled,
while the city's poor devour the entrails of swine.
Under the watchtower of the jail,
in front of its needle-pointed railings,
my first salute is from a dancing, tweed-coated, toothless man,
'Well boss?' he says, as he waltzes alone.
His name is Raymond Troy,
but known, to all, since the day he was born,
as Bisto.
Caruso arms outstretched, he sways, and sings a ballad of
his own making:

'This street was named after the Lord Lieutenant,
he visited, just once, when we'd landlords and tenants,
the son of a Tory, he became a Whig,
this majestic boulevard's famous for the pig.

A writer and Dandy by temperament,
too honest for politics,
they say he was the last of the true romantics.'

'*Oh Normanby's street has everything,*
markets to sell butter, pigs and hay,
a battery, to keep the natives at bay,
a cobbled yard to drill young men,
sent out to die for Empire and King.
It has Early Houses for the thirsty and loveless,
a boot factory for the shoeless,
a jail to punish the poor,
a tea importer, a headstone maker,
a dusty flour mill for the baker,
a rope-walk for making a noose,
a fair-green with frisky horses and wild cattle on the loose,
a mad house, if you're not right in the head,
a spacious graveyard for when you're dead.'

The whole town knows Bisto,
he drank a spinster aunt's farm,
40 good acres, with frontage, near Ballybricken;
in the rats from drink, but well enough,
to be let out each morning from the lunatic asylum.
In his surgeon's hand, the singing, waltzing Pierrot,
clenches a crumpled paper twist
to cargo coins of silver and copper,
when he heads to Mousey Delaney,
the blind huxter.

Bisto's scribbled list doesn't vary much,
a golden pimple necked quart of Lucozade,
for poor demented Jackie Stritch,
a few loose Players for Mad Mary,
The Examiner for Fr Tom Tracey,
a bar of Fry's for Jimmy Morrissey,
hairclips and rouge for Michael The Lady.

When his errands are complete,
Bisto will return to Joseph's,
where strait-jacketed time
is counted by the asylum's four faced clock.
The days of ice-cold baths are long gone,
banished, like the all-seeing eyes of the Governor's panopticon,
in these more enlightened days, the tormented are treated
with wonder drugs,
talk therapy and ECT.

I continue my stroll,
nodding at a few more familiar faces,
broken men and women, whose countenances
are marked out with the crows' feet of poverty.
I pass the gaunt Victorian villas,
on the left-hand side of the street.
Boru House is my next stop, constructed in 1880 A.D.
a lofty red-bricked house, built for a horse-dealer, with notions,
just last week, an obituary in *The Times* of London revealed,
that his famous, writer daughter, was sadly deceased.

Two hundred yards up the street, just across from the Pike,
the Fair Green wall is beginning to crumble,
white, hand-painted words boldly proclaim
'Kemmy For The Council.'
I first heard of Big Jim at my grandmother's funeral,
under a black mantilla, a pillar of the community asked:
'What's that fucking Communist doing here?'
the solid stonemason stayed at the back of the cathedral,
quietly paying his respects.

I cross the forked road, continuing on my way.
My quarry, this August morning, is to find
the final resting place of
Ellen Sharkey.
Aged 53 in 1855, Ellen was the very first to be placed
under the stony loamy soil at Spital Land, location 90a.
For six years, the wealthy of the town
refused to be buried,
alongside the poor, starving and demented.
This was finally resolved by creating
separate quarters for the poor and the quality.
Who says death has no hierarchy?

Eoin Devereux is a Professor of Cultural Sociology, poet, writer and experimental musician. He teaches the module 'Creative Writers in The Community' on the MA in Creative Writing.

LIVING IRISH IN THE TWENTY-FIRST CENTURY IN UL

Sorcha de Brún

I have as many dreams for the Irish language as there are dreams themselves. One Irish word to describe a particular type of dream is *aisling*, the term used to describe the literary form practised in the visions of Aogán Ó Rathaille and other Irish poets. *Aisling* shares a soundscape with áis linn: our resource. My dream for Irish resides in that sense of a shared landscape, in a soundscape that is alive with possibilities.

Teaching Irish for me is both art and science. Artistically, I owe much of what I practise in teaching Irish to my music teachers. Organist Gerard Gillen taught me about the importance of emotion and performance. From my piano teacher, Anthony Glavin of the Royal Irish Academy of Music (RIAM), I learned about the power of imagination and the relationship between sound,

Limerick hurlers Gearóid Hegarty
and Kyle Hayes

colour and literature. I also learned much from my own students along the way, their diverse backgrounds bringing me to where I am today in UL. These experiences have led me to adopt approaches that function as frameworks in which I teach Irish language and literature.

The first of these is to allow emotion and imagination to prevail. When the student enjoys the freedom and space to express herself in Irish in a way that is meaningful to her, she can draw on her personal powers of imagination by using techniques I have developed that improve many aspects of language acquisition. Meaning is vitally important, yet meaning and interpretation must come from the student for it to have significance. Anything else may be tantamount to rote learning, a much-criticised practice in education. It is for these reasons that I believe modern and contemporary literature with its emphasis on creativity and imagination needs to be at the heart of every Irish-language course and should be the lifeblood of the language acquisition process.

The second framework I use in teaching Irish is the conceptualisation of the language and our collective imagination. A common approach in teaching Irish is to present it in its sociolinguistic context and to emphasise its importance as artefact and bearer of identity and culture. While it is important to contextualise Irish, I believe many programmes designed to teach the language have emphasised this aspect to the detriment of the acquisition of different language skills. Allowing those studying the language to experience the rich aural, oral and imaginative phenomenon that is Irish is a measure of our self-confidence as Irish speakers, our belief in others to make their own choices around questions of Irish and identity, and our maturity as a people.

My teaching may be as much about teaching thinking skills as it is about teaching words, grammar and literature. For that reason, my general approach is not to overemphasise the minority aspect of the Irish language, while acknowledging its status. *Minority language* encourages us to associate Irish with the few, whereas majority languages are associated with the many. While this is valid, I believe this categorisation is a double-edged sword with pedagogical and intellectual challenges to how we can imagine Irish as a collective. If emotion and imagination are central to learning Irish, as I believe they are, the emphasis on the minority status of Irish can serve as a distraction. I also believe it serves as an impediment to the imagination: its status as a minority language limits its place in the world at a particular point in time, and therefore, one could argue such a description has the potential to place artificial boundaries on thought in those who speak it.

In addition, the minority framework does not address the relationship of the Irish language to Irish society. If we take a long view of history, perhaps the minority status of Irish is not the most salient aspect to learning our language, or the most important element of the language itself. I consider that all languages of the world, both minority and majority, are 'languages of the universe' as they are spoken by people or have been at different points in history. Perhaps, I tell students, it is a language spoken by a relatively small number of people; but through and in Irish we experience the universe in a particular way.

There are multifarious ways in which I teach Irish, and one of those ways is by pointing out mathematical style patterns to students. Such patterns are vividly present in aspects of Irish grammar and vocabulary. Furthermore, Irish grammar is very readily conceptualised and understood by using mathematical type models as analogous aids in explaining sequences, classifications and categories. Indeed, there are grammatical exceptions in Irish that seem chaotic; however, a reminder to students that chaos has its own proto-logic usually opens the door of understanding followed by a greater acceptance of grammatical difficulties that require a degree of experimentation and trial and error.

My interdisciplinary approach to teaching Irish that borrows from science, maths and music amongst other subjects blurs the rigid lines sometimes reflected in specialisation approaches to the Irish language. There is much to gain from interdisciplinary approaches to Irish-language teaching, learning and scholarship, pedagogically and philosophically. If we consider the often-binary positioning of science, technology, engineering and mathematics (STEM) and arts subjects, I counter this by positing that, for example, all language is as fundamental to understanding mathematics, as mathematics is to understanding language.

In a seminal essay, philosopher Richard Rorty discusses how 'democratic institutions may once again be made to serve social justice' (1998). I do not believe it is incompatible to disagree with a utilitarian approach to Irish, while at the same time expecting that language teachers respond to the needs of society. Indeed, one could argue that concern for the future of Irish and its dwindling number of native speakers behoves us to do so. For me, part of that concept of justice in successful teaching and pedagogy is rooted in trust and hope, high expectations for all students, and the fostering of confidence with colleagues and students. Some of the most interesting developments in modern

Irish since coming to the University of Limerick have involved interfaculty projects where those human qualities have been to the forefront. The Dánner-stag project, with Gisela Holfter and myself as leaders, entails the translation of numerous poems from German to Irish. The end of derogation of the Irish language in the European Union is another watershed moment for our Irish language. A final year research project supervisee has published the results of her research in an academic journal; several others have completed collections of stories and novels in Irish; and a Gaeltacht supervisee has made a significant contribution to The Irish Longitudinal Study of Ageing (TILDA) on senior citizens in Gaeltacht areas. Some of the most rewarding moments have come in quieter, less dramatic ways. In 2020, a group of fourth-year students came together, composed a piece of music for me and presented that composition to me as a finished artwork on embroidered linen. Such unexpected, private and precious gifts, given without fanfare or promotion, are amongst the most fulfilling of experiences to date in UL.

My teaching vision has always been transparent and inclusive. All students are equally treated and welcomed openly in my classes, irrespective of any prior connection with the language. My dream is always to return Irish to people in an inclusive way, and to share it as an áis, or resource, to every student who wishes to learn or speak it. The study of modern Irish offers the possibility to teach Irish to a young, increasingly confident and mature student body in a way that reflects an Ireland in transition. Modern Irish, I believe, must be rooted in, and connected to, the contemporary. Part of that zeitgeist is inclusion, diversity and equality. UL is the perfect place to realise these dreams for our living Irish language.

Dr Sorcha de Brún, a Lecturer in Modern Irish at UL, is also a poet, a musician and an award-winning writer of fiction in Irish.

TAKING UP SPACE

Sandrine Uwase Ndahiro

I first came to UL in 2014 to study for a Bachelor's degree in English and History. I remember being hyper-aware that I was the only student of African descent (Rwandan-Irish) on my course. I viewed my dual identity as a weakness. I stood out in all my classes and did not look like any of the other students or any of my lecturers or tutors. This hyper-awareness of my dual identity meant that I had a very skewed view of my place in my course and academia. The lack of representation meant that I never thought that I could one day progress into academia.

The feeling of not belonging was so strong. It all changed when I entered my undergraduate final year and came across the module 'Contemporary African Literature in English' taught by Dr Yianna Liatsos, who later became my supervisor for both my MA and PhD. I clearly remember this being the first time in my whole college experience when I felt that I had found my voice in academia. It was the first time that my African identity was celebrated and cherished. I was exposed to various African lived experiences portrayed by Africanists themselves. I was learning to critically analyse and recognise theoretical concepts from a multitude of Africanists who ranged from countries like South Africa, Kenya and Nigeria. In this class, I was exposed to African theorists like Franz Fanon, Aime Césaire and Leopold Senghor, pioneers in African studies whose works instilled in me the desire to learn more about my cultural background.

Africanists that I was being exposed to in this class were engaging with debates about stereotypes, Africanness, whiteness and the long-lasting violent history of colonialism, issues that I had always been interested in exploring but lacked the necessary tools to dissect. Taking this class cemented the functionality of literary theory as a life skill that goes beyond the classroom. The module exposed me to how my lived realities of having a dual identity enabled me to connect with these theories on much deeper and intimate levels. Through the module, I gained a more in-depth understanding of my cultural heritage and confidence to be a researcher and to have a voice in academia.

As part of this module, I learned about the history of Rwanda and the 1994 genocide. I was able to discover so much about my history while simultaneously growing critical awareness of a topic that was so personal to me. Rwanda's history through the lens of African literature exposed me to a new way of approaching the long-lasting colonial effects across the African continent. Before coming to UL, the information I had about Rwanda was always under a homogenous lens that projected the stereotype of all Africans being barbaric savages in dire need of Western intervention. The constant stereotypes that were projected onto those from Africa, especially coming from a country that was known for its recent violent history, meant that I had a disconnect with my Rwandan heritage. Taking Dr Liatsos's class made me aware of African literary works that acted as counter-narratives to the dominant European and American coverage of the Rwandan genocide. I saw the power of changing narratives and taking charge of my own narrative. The module espoused the power of African literature but, more specifically, the benefits of taking an interdisciplinary approach to both Western and African schools of thought.

Having the opportunity to take modules on contemporary African literature and postcolonial literature exposed me to the dichotomy and tension between the Global North and Global South. In these classes, I was able to further my interest in stereotypes projected onto African characters that are visible in popular culture, NGO advertisements, film, music, the list is endless. I noticed that through these dehumanising projections, the African characters' sense of humanity and unique lived realities were either ignored or just reduced to mere objects. This constant depiction left me feeling determined to change the narrative by solely using African cultural texts that represent the African characters as singularly unique individuals. Through this quest, I was constantly elevating a better understanding of my African cultural and historical backgrounds. I found that I was becoming more confident in my academic skills but also becoming unapologetically Rwandan-Irish.

Studying at UL gave me the space to pick and choose modules that matched my interests and passions. Constant engagement with such modules paved the way for me to confidently delve into questions of ethnicity, race, cultural and social representation in both the Global South and Global North. For the first time, my African heritage, fluency and knowledge of Swahili, a language spoken by more than 100 million Africans, gave me a linguistic advantage that makes me stand out as a young African-Irish scholar, a title that I never thought was possible.

As I progress further into my PhD, I have noticed that my passion for offering alternative ways to approach the African continent and its people is continuously growing. My dissertation offers a postcolonial reading of the scholarly discourse of the Anthropocene, which stipulates humankind as the agent of climate change and the sixth mass extinction. The West still views contemporary Africa as a place that showcases a series of historical experiences of suffering, like transatlantic slavery, colonialism and apartheid. Climate change is viewed as another in the long list of issues already affecting this 'unstable' continent. My research through the lens of the Anthropocene and futurity hopes to trouble this oversimplified manner of overlooking climate change issues that are disproportionately affecting African countries. My thesis thus offers a postcolonial reading of the environmental crisis by highlighting an alternative understanding of the climate crisis from an Africanist perspective. I use cultural texts like fiction, non-fiction, film and art to reveal how contemporary Africanists are bearing witness to the ongoing environmental issues like extractivism, drought and pollution, by centralising Africans' intimate relationship with the natural world. My chosen cultural texts inform an alternative way of understanding climate change by recognising local knowledge, production and solutions in an African context. Through my field of study, I am in the unique position of disseminating the concept of 'futurity' that will contribute to current debates about climate change from a distinctive African and Irish perspective, a perspective that I view as crucial.

As I am approaching eight years in UL, I can see how my love for centralising African voices has also been adapted into a non-academic setting. As a Black woman in academia, I have had to work extremely hard to be in a place where I am taking up space in a field that is still predominantly white. Constantly reflecting on how far I have come has equipped me with skills I have been able to adapt and use to make a change in minority communities. My love for literature and taking charge of telling my own story inspired me to create a new interdisciplinary literary and cultural magazine called *Unapologetic*. I, alongside my co-editors Gareth Brinn and Professor Margaret Harper, have a vision in creating a safe space where those from marginalised communities have a platform where they can explore what it means to be unapologetic.

My time in UL has allowed me to grow and become unapologetically Afro-Irish when taking an interdisciplinary approach in my research, creative and activist work. My constant public engagement work that looks at the changing nature of Irishness in fields like literature and film allows me to proudly pave the way for young Black scholars to help shape the Irish cultural landscape.

Through my research, I am hoping to achieve my dream of aligning myself with this school of thought by reworking the future temporality from an African cultural perspective that will further the conversation both in postcolonial/ Africanist studies and, more widely, within the field of environmental studies and ecocriticism.

Lastly, one of the proudest moments that I have had in UL was the opportunity to give a guest lecture in the African Literature module. When I was in my first year, I never thought that I would stand in front of students teaching a topic that I loved. It proved to be an out-of-body experience as a young Black scholar teaching the importance of African literature. This opportunity just reminded me how far I have come while also acting as a further push to continuously expose students to an alternative understanding of theorists from an African perspective as the Western school of thought is constantly the default theory. From this moment onwards I have seen that it is possible for me to take up space as I belong in academia.

A leader of the journal Unapologetic, *Sandrine Ndahiro, a graduate of the MA in English, is currently completing her PhD studies at the School of English, Irish, and Communication.*

DÚICHE

—

Anna Ryan Moloney

I t is the first day of my new job, and I am late. I spent a while poring over my foldout map of Limerick city last night, while staying at my friend's house in Corbally, and decided to cycle this Brigid's Day morning along the River Shannon to get to UL. My purple Raleigh carried me for many student years around the hills of Cork city and now, in clothes newly purchased to make a professional impression, I pedal the morning-sharp air between black-bare trees. A dense fog sits cold and low on the heaving breadth of river-water. The rising sun strains the air. Each humpback bridge, each trail-bend, is a surprise on this riverbank journey of discovery, one that is taking longer than I expected. The new clothes feel awkward, a version of myself I don't know. I find my way and arrive. Invigorated. River-fresh. Late.

In responding to the invitation to write about the architecture and spaces of the UL campus, I have found myself tracing memories, retaking journeys. This piece has become a collage of repeated spatial encounters with spaces that are woven through my lived experience of the campus over the fifteen years I have worked here. Inevitably, I must leave out more than I can include. (For an historical account of the architecture and development of UL, see David Fleming's *The University of Limerick: A History*, 2012). Travelling to the campus, from the various houses I have lived in, has been central to how I have come to understand the spaces of the university, its city, its people and its contexts. That is where I begin.

Year One: I live off the South Circular Road. The Childers Road is my route to work. As a child, I travelled this road many times each year, on our journey from Dublin to my mom's homeplace. Childers Road held a very particular stage of the journey. From the back seat of our Opel Ascona I watched out for Chadwicks, as it meant we would soon stop at the traffic lights and turn left. This turn felt momentous, a gateway that indicated to us, in our excitement, that Abbeyfeale, my uncles and the farm were getting much nearer. Now this road is my twice-daily passage through the lives of the Limerick communities that meet it, from the Hyde Road and Ballinacurra, from Roxborough and the edges of Southill.

Year Two: I live near Monaleen where cattle fields meet motorway meet housing. My daily walk to work is the undulating ridge of the Golf Links Road. From its summit, I connect in rotation: with the Galtees and Ballyhouras to the south, the city to the west, and the gentle hills of Clare to the north, as I descend into the stretch of river-bend land on which the university has been placed. On past the weight of Seán Scully's stone abstraction and the beacons of wind-singing flagpoles. Into the territory of the river, low and flat.

Year Three: I settle in the city centre, on the north side. First in a cluster of riverside brick houses, and then one block back from the breadth of its flow where I can hear the cascade of the Curragower Falls at low tide as its rise and fall measures time. Where river-shallow waters mingle with salt journeying to and from the ocean, as I cross the stone bridge, over and over. The browns

and reds of the clay from its estuarine banks form the brick-grid of the city – a city grown from the ambition of a pink-hued eighteenth-century drawing of speculative expansion, layered on the topography of fertile river-edge. I cycle to work along the river, its slow-moving surface concealing a weighty energy pulling beneath. Sometimes swollen by rain. Sometimes sparkling, dispersing, reforming. Each twist of the journey is now intimately familiar. At the Black Bridge, I take the sudden right, down the speed-swoop of mud-hill, through the high growth. Occasionally, I cross that bridge and follow the network of small roads that wander by rolling fields, towards the East Clare territory of my dad's childhood in Sallybank, the glacial landscape between Truagh and Broadford.

Year Ten: I live upstream, where the expanse of Lough Derg funnels itself into river. I watch winter morning fog sit low on the lake, dissipating with the slow-growing warmth of the day. The moon lingers high as its fullness lights dark mornings. I trace the colours of trees and hedges that rise on the hills, changing through the passing of each month, each year. The river is soft-edged as the water seeps and surges towards the sea. The late summer sun tumbles behind Moylussa, into a fiery-pink sky. I journey to work parallel to the banks of Ardnacrusha's headrace, passing the point where the water, for almost a century, has split in two. The smooth-surfaced canal prepares itself to power the country. The remaining river meanders, gathering debris around small islands through Castleconnell, the Falls of Doonass, the university.

I am twenty-something again, a fresh graduate of architecture in UCD. I am with my sister and dad, meeting his good friend from their hillwalking days – the late John O'Connor. With infectious enthusiasm, John walks us across the yet-to-be-opened road bridge that will connect the Limerick campus with my dad's home county. I sense windswept openness, prospect and potential, and John's animated description of energetic plans for the university's expansion. Little do I know that I will, one day, become part of that story; that I will stand beneath this same bridge with my own first-year architecture students, as they design and construct structures with timber laths, celebrating qualities of space and light in the undercroft of folded concrete.

I sit with my back to Plassey House, facing directly south, on one of the three benches in the courtyard wrapped by the concrete skeleton and brown mass of the main building. The sun reaches into the outdoor room with its herringbone red-brick ground, its swathe of smooth-sloping grass and its Monterey Cypress, strapped and belted against any oncoming storm. My eyes close to the blinding of sun-strong light, the sound of fountain water-rush, the drops of wind-splash. An intensity of the moment.

I step from gravel-crunch, up worn-smooth stone steps, push open the timber-heavy door and enter the calm spaciousness of Plassey House, into the easy comfort of the East Room, with its former layout of winged chairs and couches, teacups and plates of biscuits. Informal formality.

I pass the stand of trees and swell of lawn, down towards the original piece

of twentieth-century architecture on the campus – the PESS building – with its fabulous geometries and hooded eyelids concealing its ventilation. Like an animal stretching itself by the riverbank, its north façade is in conversation with the trees as its overcoat of shingles accumulates the damp-green patina of age.

I gaze at the President's House, designed by Grafton Architects. This tower-house is sentinel on the riverbank, a three-dimensional lived-in sculpture.

I sit in the hush of the nest-like space on the top floor of the library, the old home of Special Collections. With glass-fronted cabinets, bookrests and pencils, a doorway to hidden archives of precious volumes, these rooms hold rituals and materials befitting their name. Beyond, the other library spaces are glass-quiet, sealed above the buzz of the university grounds. Spaces caught between bookshelves frame views across treetops.

I close my eyes and listen to the swell of music in the Tower Theatre, its circular drum shaping a special intimacy between performers and audience.

I sit in my office, on the top floor of the Engineering Research Building, looking west, high across the city, to the beacon of St Mary's Cathedral, to the curves of Thomond Park. The afternoon light mingles with the sounds of chattering below. Occasionally I stick my head out the window to enjoy the spectacle.

I navigate the labyrinth of the main building, towards the stair core of the C block. Everyone looks down, eyes watching the steps, as though the tiles on the stair-treads are demanding attention. Voices echo upwards, buffeted by the heaviness of sand-blasted concrete, its rough loveliness highlighted by the light raking through the angled glass on each landing.

I sit at desk after desk, beside student after student, year after year, discussing drawings and models, the spirit of their proposals as they design alternative futures. The studio of the School of Architecture: an unexpected space entered through an unassuming door labelled CG-042 – the physical space a demonstration of the conceptual process of design. I try not to take for granted the energy, creativity and potential that emerges within this space, generated by the students that inhabit it with such passion.

In the offices immediately beside and below me there are journalists, scientists, novelists, architects, engineers and scholars of language and literature. I relish the togetherness of this diversity and appreciate it as the privilege of working in this university.

Dr Anna Ryan Moloney is a Lecturer in the UL School of Architecture. In 2022/23 she took an MA in Creative Writing at UL.

THE PINK LADIES

Manon Gilbart

L ooking through the glazed facade of the Plaza Café, I watch students and staff buzzing around UL's busiest spot. As people walk in and out of the library, five ladies dressed in bright pink uniforms are restlessly working behind the counter. Despite the vibrant pace of the place, each customer is greeted with the same heart-warming enthusiasm.

Everyone knows the Pink Ladies. Not only do they serve coffee, but they also offer lively conversation to anyone who walks through the door. Something we all desperately needed after the numerous lockdowns.

Walking past the Library Café, it is hard not to stop to say 'Hi' to Geraldine Sheahan, Lee Tynan, Marian Kennedy, Mary Egan and Siobhán Carr. Over a cup of coffee, I get to chat with them.

The Plaza opened its doors in 1997. Geraldine has been working there for quite some time, as she is one of the original staff members. 'It will be twenty-four years soon. My youngest boy was six at the time, he will be twenty-nine next February, that's how long I've been here.'

She believes that the interactions she has with the students are different from those with the general public because of their age. 'They're free and carefree, they're a lovely bunch.'

Geraldine speaks highly of her fellow Pink Ladies. 'When you come in in the morning, you have a bit of a laugh before you start, it makes things easier.'

Because of their motherly presence, the students often refer to the Pink Ladies as mammies. After chatting with them, I begin to understand why.

Marian loves working in the Plaza, mostly due to the atmosphere of the place. 'It's like one big happy family. The kids, the students, they're lovely. It's like they're your kids, and you're like the mother that's minding them and making sure they're all okay.'

After a pause, she adds: 'You just go through all the stages with them, you can feel their emotions. You know when they're sad, when they're stressed, when they need that little bit of a pick me up in the morning just to get them going. It doesn't take anything else of your day to be pleasant, to be good to people.'

According to the other Pink Ladies, Mary has an infectious laugh which instantly puts a smile on their faces. I get to hear it when she explains to me how they can't stay apart.

'You know, we'd be joking and say we need a break from each other. But even when we're off, we still meet up for tea or coffee because we do miss each other.'

When she comes into work, Mary looks forward to meeting 'the girls' and having chats with the students. 'I like to see how they're doing, how their day is going. Sometimes the week goes by, and you're checking in, who's in and who's not.'

'I'm always extra nice to people because I don't know what's going on in their life. I feel like nobody bothers to check in on each other anymore. Take a few minutes to check in with people.'

Mary often wonders where the students are, where they ended up. 'I love when some of them come here and get jobs or come back to do a Master's or a PhD. I'd love to travel around the world and see how many students I could meet. I know a lot of them went off to Canada and Australia.'

Siobhán, who started working in the Plaza three years ago, often wondered if some of the students would return after the lockdown.

'You'd miss them, you're so used to them coming in. Some of them are in a relationship, and you know, you'd be wondering if they are still together. We look out for them. It could be anyone's child, you'd be scared that they'd go the wrong path.'

Lee has worked in the Plaza for almost seven years, and she cooks hearty meals for both the staff and the students every day. Speaking of her co-workers, she says: 'The thing is, everybody is warm and friendly, we work very well as a team. Everybody is supportive, and I've always found that when I had a few ups and downs, they're just a rock. It's like having an extended family.'

She takes pride in the way the Pink Ladies treat everyone in the same manner. Lee believes that at the end of the day, kindness is all that matters. 'I think it's terribly important. We do our best just to be nice, pleasant, and to always be supportive.'

Recently, a post from UL Confessions, the anonymous site where UL students tweet, received hundreds of likes on Twitter. It read: 'May sound cringe but f*ck it, the ladies working in the Library canteen deserve some sort of honorary medal from UL for how nice they are, I genuinely believe they brighten up everyone who goes into that canteen's day!'

After sitting down with each of them, I have noticed that the tales of the Pink Ladies and their work environment are often intertwined. As a motherly atmosphere reigns, it is easy to see why everyone feels at home in the Plaza.

'Do you want another coffee, pet?' asks Marian after noticing my nearly empty cup. 'Did you have something to eat this morning, are you sure you're not hungry?'

From Belgium, Manon Gilbart is a graduate of UL Journalism. Geraldine Sheahan, Lee Tynan, Marian Kennedy, Mary Egan and Siobhán Carr enhance the well-being of the UL community every day through their work at the Library Café.

LIVE MUSIC IS A BRIDGE

Ber Angley

(in conversation with Eoin Devereux)

I started out in the entertainment sector in the late 1970s. I used to help the late Brendan Murray organise events in the old Savoy Complex on Henry Street. As we came to the end of that decade, I met NIHE student John Ryan, who subsequently became Mayor of Limerick. He said he needed help to organise gigs at NIHE. At this time, I was also helping to put on shows in Mary I and in the Art College in Limerick. I was based in the Union of Students in Ireland (USI) regional office in a basement in Cecil Street. I have fond memories of myself and Tim Nolan popping over to Flan Costello's for tea.

At NIHE, there was very little activity on campus, but the Entertainments Officer, folk musician Barry Moore, who would later become Luka Bloom, organised an occasional show in the Swift Lecture Theatre. The first show I organised with John Ryan took place in the old canteen. Back then, it was a prefab and was located on the site now occupied by the Analog Devices Building. The first gig we organised featured a UK reggae group, Icarus. We soon moved to the new canteen, where Red Raisins is situated now, putting on gigs by groups such as Southpaw, The Atrix, Berlin and Lene Lovich.

In the 1980s I started to organise events on my own on an ad-hoc basis. This led to me being hired by the ULSU as their entertainments co-ordinator. I set up a student-led Ents crew to assist with gigs. The first crew I assembled included the now Sinn Féin Senator Paul Galvin and Clare fiddler Martin Hayes of The Gloaming.

Most of our gigs were on campus. We used the canteen, EGO10 and the student centre in the Stables Courtyard. There were just two full-time elected officers in the Students' Union and two staff members, Carmel Carey and myself. In addition to Ents, I also worked on student publications and helped with clubs and societies. I started the Theatre Workshop, Campus Television, the Photography and Softball societies.

In the mid-1980s I organised many more events and put on a lot of free lunchtime concerts in the Student Centre. In this, I was helped by the great composer Patrick Cassidy. These featured many renowned artists, including Mary Black. By 1983, we began to organise gigs in the city. Starting in the Glentworth Hotel, we also made use of the entire Savoy complex. Our shows included performances by In Tua Nua, Aslan and Stockton's Wing. Stockton's Wing attracted more than 3,200 punters.

With the advent of The Stables, I focused on offering a wider entertainment service. With the support of the SU officers, we set up a non-commercial unit to benefit the students, so when money was made, it was ploughed back into putting on free events such as fun sports events and free films at the weekend. My aim here was to build a better sense of community amongst the student population.

In 1985 I decided, with the SU vice-president Chris McInerney (now a Senior Lecturer in the UL Department of Politics and Public Administration) and Paddy McPoland (IT Carlow and now a tour manager), to go to London

to meet with music agents, with the view to expanding the scope of our gig offerings. As a result, I set up the Irish College Circuit, so that we could organise nationwide tours for visiting acts. Our first UL show featured the Deep Sea Jivers, Rent Party and The Lotus Eaters, in EGO10. By then, I was also working with Irish music promoters such as MCD, Louis Walsh and Pat Egan. It was through my work with Pat Egan that I was able to book Billy Connolly to perform in EGO10. I also organised the first ever shows by Johnny Cash and Kris Kristofferson at the UCH.

In my capacity at ULSU Ents officer, I was responsible for putting on gigs by performers including 808 State, The Christians, Opus 3, Technotronic, The Stunning, The Blades, Clannad, Christy Moore, The Wedding Present, Carter USM, Ultrasonic, Jo Brand and Therapy? Perhaps my proudest achievement, however, was my decision to book The Cranberries.

It was 1991 when I put on the first show by The Cranberries, initially as a support act and then as a headline act in The Stables. The Cranberries were going from strength to strength, and we featured them at ULSU gigs in The Parkway, Two Mile Inn, Jetland Centre and finally their major homecoming show in The Theatre Royal on 17 December 1993.

I really enjoyed my time as Ents Officer at UL. I still meet UL alumni from all over the world who speak fondly of the gigs they attended. Looking back at my time spent on the campus I would say that my main objective was to bring students together. I tried to achieve this through Campus TV, through organising Mystery Trains to far-flung towns, by DJing in The Stables and, most of all, by organising live music gigs. Of all of these, live music has been the bridge by which students connected with one another. It's how memories are made. These days when I stand at the coffee-counter end of The Stables I can still hear a faint trace of The Cranberries first performing their songs 'Linger' and 'Dreams'.

In 2018, DJ and documentary maker Ber Angley was honoured by the City of Limerick for his hugely important role in the local and university music scene since the 1980s.

LONESOME TONIGHT:
THE MUSIC OF FRANK McCOURT

Joseph O'Connor

It was in a theatre – the old Irish Arts Centre on 51st Street in Manhattan – that I first met Frank McCourt. He was there because he was appearing in the New York premiere of a play of mine, *Red Roses and Petrol*, in a role that required some singing. It was delightfully obvious to me from the start, as it was to everyone who knew him, that Frank was a man who loved performance and song, the smell of the greasepaint, the roar of the crowd, but also the gentler consolations afforded by music in a troubled and uncertain world.

He had trod the boards himself, with his brother Malachy and others. But his conversation sparkled in a special way when he was talking about song, the Irish ballads, come-all-ye's and lullabies of his Limerick childhood, as well as the jazz standards and classics of the great American songbook, those shimmering numbers done by Ella Fitzgerald and Frank's adored Billie Holiday, full of zizzing violins, blowsy brass and the steam of sultry Manhattan. It was one of the things that made him such wonderful company. An evening with Frank was like being in the company of a beautiful jukebox.

Songs sprinkle themselves with likeable prodigality throughout Frank's books, too, but particularly throughout his debut, the phenomenally successful instant classic *Angela's Ashes*, the most widely translated Irish memoir of all time. It's a book featuring a repertoire that encompasses dozens and dozens of songs: everything from 'The Green Glens of Antrim', 'The West's Awake', 'Roddy McCorley', 'Oh, The Nights of the Kerry Dancing' to 'Kevin Barry', and from there to a different but no less heartfelt sort of lament, Elvis Presley's 'Are You Lonesome Tonight?'

Frank's characters see songs as passport and pillow: portal into a better world of dreaminess and hope, and, simultaneously, consolation for the actual life they are living. His writing has a sort of soundtrack, as most lives do. Often, we remember ourselves by reference to song: the summer of our first love, the winter someone emigrated, the troubled times and happier ones, the downs and the ups, a personal songbook put together by each of us in close collaboration with that most bittersweet of co-writers, Fate. Frank's characters are always aware of that connection. Often, they don't have a choice.

And there is music, too, in Frank's prose itself. Like all good writers, he knew that words are sounds before they are anything else. For that reason, his writing is so full of zest and naughtiness and playfulness and heart, so attuned to the juiciness of popular speech. And he knew that words can stir all the physical senses. A lovely thing about Frank was that he adored the food writing of MFK Fisher, for example, and her ability to render food so palatable you could taste it. Perhaps only someone who had known hunger could love plenitude so beautifully described. But Frank loved all words as music.

Reviewing *Angela's Ashes* for *Le Monde* on 5 September 1997, John McGahern wrote, 'In the language, in the style, McCourt has crafted a language culled from many sources: prayers, blasphemy, poetry, song, slang, Church doctrine, the cinema and much else,' before going on to salute the book's 'tones of irony and ribald laughter as well as defiance'. He concluded, 'It is a wonderfully enjoyable and moving work.' Any of the millions of readers of *Angela's Ashes* will know exactly what McGahern meant. It is as though Frank had toiled away at some massive cathedral organ of the English language, particularly that beautifully adaptable and nuanced version of it as it is spoken in Limerick, pulling out every stop, using every sound available, to bring his tale of two cities to life.

We hear in Frank's work a particular quality of musicality that we hear, in different ways, in the writings of Synge, O'Casey and Dickens, a trio of major writers with whose work Frank's own has important things in common. It can be no coincidence that two of those great figures are best known for playwriting and that the third was such a gifted theatrical performer of his writing that his audiences would often be spellbound. Indeed, a deep awareness of that sense of entertainment and not just art survives into many people's favourite musical, Lionel Bart's classic Dickens adaptation, *Oliver!* Frank's writing, similarly, while it is beautiful and funny on the page, has something in it that wants to be announced, performed, sung out; shared in the particular way that the presence of a live audience generates. Indeed, it is entirely appropriate that *Angela's Ashes* is now a musical, the form, perhaps, towards which it was always evolving, even as it delighted its millions of readers. The music was always there, as it is there in the work of all the best writers, who know you might be lonesome tonight.

Joseph O'Connor is Frank McCourt Chair of Creative Writing. His novels have been published in forty languages. In 2022 he received the American Ireland Funds AWB Vincent Literary Award.

KEEPING IT COUNTRY

Aileen Dillane

Genre is a funny thing; in music, anyway. It's not just about how a song or piece of music is structured, sounded and rendered in a particular style. It extends into the social, the ideological, the political, and so much more. The genres of music one produces or consumes are understood to be intimately bound with who you are and how you render yourself musically. They become a question of taste and of values. Some genres are seen as part of High Art, others are connected to low art or subcultures (yes, the use of capitals is deliberate).

Polarising positions on genre are valuable to unpick for so many reasons, but especially as an educator. What is at stake when you follow one kind of music instead of another? Who are the arbiters of taste? What is 'worth' learning about, canonising, and what genres do not have intrinsic 'value'? As

Johnny Cash and Kris Kristofferson at the University Concert Hall.

an ethnomusicologist I would say all genres are worth studying, not because I'm a relativist, but because, when I suspend my own taste and look at 'why' people follow certain kinds of musics and, importantly, how they become part of their social (or indeed interior) lives, then I'm learning so much about society; who is included and excluded; what the music signifies for those that produce/consume it or criticise it; how its practices and discourses are enacted and shaped; what it tells us about humanity, for music, according to the eminent ethnomusicologist John Blacking 'is humanly organised sound'. For most cultures, this is true. Music is intentional. It accompanies rites and rituals. It is part of lived experience, penetrating all aspects of our lives. *Music as Social Life* goes the title of a book by Thomas Torino.

Armed with all of these thoughts, I decided it was time UL had a special module entitled 'Narratives and Sounds of Country Music'. So I proposed it. My reasons were multifold. Ground-breaking television programmes like *Bringing It All Back Home* in the 1990s had shown the strong transatlantic connection between traditions in Ireland (and Scotland) and the United States, especially in Appalachia. Irish balladry and country music from the USA were cousins. So too were bluegrass and Irish dance music. It took me a while to understand that lots of other cultures were largely excluded from this narrative initially, including African-American slaves who brought the banjo and laments to America. But even that was a valuable lesson because the 'whiteness' of country music would also be something I would address in the class.

The day the module went before Academic Council there was, I learned second hand, some degree of mirth when my proposal came up for discussion. 'Sniggering' was the word actually used. I suppose country music might have seemed like an unusual topic for serious study to some. But on reading my aims and objectives and the associated peer-reviewed literature, with a throat clearing and a consensus, the module was entered in the canon of offerings at UL. I did wait to hear if there was a caveat of no line-dancing on campus, but that did not materialise, thankfully.

I was around fifteen when I first started playing what one might call 'Country and Irish' music. It was that genre that blended Irish traditional music with different aspects of balladry, occasionally in a country style. For me it was simply Irish songs and tunes. I gigged with a local musician at weddings and céilithe, playing dance tunes and singing songs from Ireland and the English folk tradition, and the States. These days Country and Irish is more defined, thanks to programmes like *Viva Ceol Tíre* or *Stetsons and Stilettos* on Irish stations. But what I did learn is that those listening and dancing loved the four-square blend, doing the two-step as much as doing a Kerry set, and enjoying a social life that was not limited by boundaries of genre or the imagination.

For our very first class with BA in Irish Music and Dance students, we went through the syllabus carefully. 'We're learning about Dolly Parton?' one student exclaimed in excitement. 'Yes,' was my answer. 'There is so much to learn about how she positions herself as a performer and woman in this genre.' As they pored over the syllabus, each thematic week supported by growing international scholarship in the area, they quickly latched on to the fact that I was taking them on a field trip.

The Greenhills Hotel in Caherdavin on the outskirts of Limerick City had long been a host to various Irish and international country music stars. We were going for a night out, to have a first-hand experience of listening to the music, engaging in dancing, studying the social context, taking note of the discourse, recording the list of songs and any other participant-observations. One young woman in the class 'came out' and said, 'I actually love this music and go dancing at least once a week, but I don't tell too many people.' Shame of a genre of music can be a hard thing to negotiate. Others were trepidatious, wondering if they'd have to say yes if someone asked them to dance. I said no but asked them to pay particular attention to the culture and the dynamic of these exchanges, noting that 'the lovely girl' syndrome was alive and well in many genres of dance music, but especially those more associated with conservative positions, as seemed evident in the literature we were reading. On the night, the students fully engaged, mostly women and one man. We had an incredible discussion afterwards in the next class. They had wonderful theories about the connections between the Irish lament, the high lonesome of country, the rhizomatic tendrils of migration that shape musics across the globe. They surmised why country in Ireland is so often associated with farming and GAA. They were surprised to learn of how the Red Cow Hotel in Dublin is a hotbed of country and how more people in Ireland at that time listened to country on radio more than any other genre. We went on to explore Aboriginal Australian country musicians and festivals and uncovered the less spoken about African-American country singers and cowboys who get written out of the main narrative. Why? we asked over and over. Why?

The class lasted a few more years but changes in elective offerings within a restricted bundle meant that there was never again enough of a critical mass to run the module. Instead, I transferred aspects of it into my first year Introduction to Popular Music and Dance. Opportunities to talk about 'Old Town Road' by Lil Nas X are simply too important to let slide – a queer, African-American man taking the conservative country music charts by storm? What is at stake? Why is this important? What does it tell us about identity, power and privilege through music? And when Garth Brooks sells out multiple shows in Dublin, isn't it important that students know about his fame in the 1990s and how, for a while, primary schools switched out PE classes for line-dancing? Don't students still need to understand and critique how genre can be aligned with collective politics and how country music and white ethnonationalism can be bedfellows but also how musicians and audiences can wrest the music from that narrative and make it their own? Music is polysemous. It is the stuff of dreams. Genre is simply structure. *We make meaning.*

Dr Aileen Dillane is a musician, educator and researcher. Aileen co-directs UL's Centre for the Study of Popular Music and Popular Culture. She plays flute, piano and bouzouki.

KATE O'BRIEN IN SPECIAL COLLECTIONS

Kathy Rose O'Brien

I'm hunched over a tiny, century-old photograph of my protagonist, wondering if I squint would it be possible to time-travel for a second. I lock eyes with her, but she is trapped in her sepia environs. I want to find a way to meet this woman. It's why I'm here.

I fantasised that proximity to some of her things might conjure her up. There are diaries and postcards, even a playbill that would have rested in her lap at the opening night of *Esperando a Godot* in Madrid. Is it enough to make me a medium?

I have noted the themes in her novels and heard her voice on recordings but who she is remains faint to me, like the photograph, faded by time. I'm an actor by profession, trained to look for points of connection between myself and a role. In the quest for information about a character, the actor mines the text.

My first question is always: 'What does the character say about *herself*?'

In UL's Glucksman Library, I'm researching the twentieth-century Irish writer Kate O'Brien for an exhibition about her at a soon-to-open museum of literature in Dublin. I have yet to reveal, to myself or anyone else, what aspect of her life or work the exhibition will focus on. In front of me in Special Collections, an even more hushed, more exalted precinct of the Glucksman Library, a wall of grey archive boxes yields photographs and manuscripts, letters and ephemera pertaining to my Limerick muse. Behind them a portrait of Kate O'Brien hangs by the door. After digesting the contents of a box it is returned to the storage vault. It is surely an archivist's joke that as the grey wall comes down, O'Brien comes stealthily into view. It is not proving so simple. I contemplate burying my face in one of the manuscript pillows and screaming.

I resist and instead focus on finding out what my heroine says about herself. She wrote columns, the archive list tells me. I move my attention from photographic to literary material, pencilling in the corresponding numbers under the classification 'Articles' on the request form. When the box arrives there's an *Evening Standard* article on top from 1928, entitled 'Do Independent Women Make the Best Wives?' Journalist O'Brien believes yes, working women do indeed. I catch my breath. Can this date be right? I'm the only researcher in the library annex but I look around incredulously all the same.

'As a good feminist I have always believed, or tried to believe, that if women had more power in government, throughout the world, then the world would be more pacifically and more sensitively run, perhaps?'

A yelp escapes me as I read the first four words of the next article, from *Creation Magazine*, but senior library assistant Jean Turner looks more intrigued than disapproving. I've spent a handful of weeks throughout the past year here and I've behaved myself up until this point.

I have free rein to steer the exhibition as I wish, but, despite being a relative, I've not been sure that I relate to this novelist, playwright and journalist. I never met Kate O'Brien. Born in Limerick in 1897, she was my grandfather's older sister and died years before my birth. I asked my father, who was close to her, if she was a feminist. He found it hard to imagine her calling herself that. It feels like a victory to clutch the typed pages of this article dated 1969 and hear her advance her proclamation further: 'Until women are to some extent in charge of the world's money, and God knows when that will be, because men are certainly alerted enough, I think, to hold that citadel, we, the females, will have no voice worth hearing in men's greedy wars.'

Spurred on by my grand-aunt, over fifty years ago, calling out the gender pay gap and lack of women in power globally, I delve further into the grey box, relishing, as she must have, the proliferation of her 'Long Distance' columns in *The Irish Times*. Her writings unnervingly resonate with the polemics of today, despite being half a century old. O'Brien, in her seventies, wrote every month or so about such topics as conservation ('Where have all the butterflies gone?'), Ireland's 'superbly male reaction against independent women' and asked the question 'Why can't we feed people on our own planet?' as filmed footage of famine was seen by a global audience for the first time in Biafra.

I'm stunned by her prescience in 1970, as she worries that plastic packaging is everywhere: 'The poor island is almost sinking beneath its monstrous load of debris … on the shores you'll see dead birds and decaying fish floating in.' I want to pull out my phone and (after I've explained what it is) show her the viral images from that very week of clogged beaches all around the world.

Our imagined conviviality continues when I hear her laugh in exasperation in the *Daily Express* in 1928, replying to a nonsensical question posed (by her editor?):

> What will women do next? What will any of us do next? If
> you were to ask me I could not tell you what I shall do next

myself, or what my cat will do next, or what my butcher's boy. How then can I guess at the future antics of trillions of people, all as different from each other as me and my cat and my butcher's boy?

I'm elated. Her modern and self-assured voice is as clear as a bell. Reading her opinion pieces alongside her fiction brings her into sharper focus. I finally have a direction for the exhibition. The last few grey boxes skirt the wall and out of a sense of duty I dip in.

'Keep this poem for me please' is scrawled in a hand I've begun to recognise, on a neat newspaper clipping in the penultimate box. It's a poem, 'No Voyage' by Mary Oliver. It's one of her first published poems, long before she won the Pulitzer Prize. I know this because I am a fan of Oliver. I never tire of 'Wild Geese', 'The Journey' or 'The Summer Day'. It's a thrill to find it amongst O'Brien's miscellany of saved bits and pieces, an idea of her other interests. Still, I look up the dates on my laptop because I can't believe that their careers overlap. It's hard for me to imagine them existing simultaneously. Am I witnessing Kate's first encounter with the poet? I hold the newspaper page as she did and read the poem. My finger traces her pen, following her decision to stake an interest in this young American scribe with instructions that her poem be saved for later. I'm so glad it was. It has been saved for me. We sit together in companionable silence, finally meeting.

Kathy Rose O'Brien is an acclaimed actor and curator. Arrow to the Heart, *her exhibition about Kate O'Brien, premiered at the Museum of Literature Ireland (MoLI) in 2020.*

'I'M NOT DOING IT!'

Olivia Fitzmaurice

S eptember 1992, a month shy of my seventeenth birthday, my parents took me to UL. Green does not even begin to describe mollycoddled number eight of nine children, me. I even brought my mother into the Jean Monnet theatre for the first induction lecture. She didn't stay.

I had been offered a place on the coveted Physical Education programme, the only one in Ireland at the time. We had to choose an elective, and we had the option of either mathematics or English. I can still remember so clearly Professor John O'Donoghue telling us that should we choose mathematics, we could stand with pride, knowing our degree would be on a par with any mathematics degree from any other university in the world. I was sold. Mathematics it was.

I loved every minute of my degree programme. I remember the late Dave Weldrick telling our class we were the *crème de la crème* of school-leaving students and believing him. Prof. O'Donoghue guided our evolution from students of mathematics to mathematics teachers. I remember leaving St Mary's school in Nenagh after my first teaching practice laden down with teddies and gifts, brimming with happiness, knowing I was on the perfect career path for me. On my graduation day in 1996, Prof. O'Donoghue told my parents, 'She will be back.' I still did not realise the profound influence he had had and would continue to have in my life.

I taught for a number of years at secondary school and found that no matter what mathematics class I taught, I was always buzzing afterwards. I felt like I would teach mathematics for free if I needed to. Most days provided some form of an epiphany. I was always learning something new or understanding something a bit better. Teaching PE didn't have the same lure for me. Since

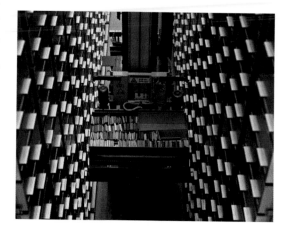

leaving UL, I had thought on and off about returning to study mathematics again. One rainy day I was standing in a sandpit, clipboard in arm, pleading with a second-year student to please attempt the long jump so I could complete a round of trials for the county athletic championships. She (I remember her name and face vividly) stood with her arms folded shouting back at me, 'I'M NOT DOING IT.' I told the principal that afternoon I had made up my mind and would be returning to college. If that girl only knew the impact she would have on my life!

I took a school group to an open day in UL and called on Prof. O'Donoghue (eventually he would be just John) for a chat. I chatted with him about returning to study, but I didn't know if it was mathematics or mathematics education I wanted to return to. He advised me to go to NUI Maynooth to complete a diploma in mathematics and that would help make my mind up. I called him again after that year and said I missed teaching mathematics and he said, 'So it is mathematics education after all.'

John offered me the opportunity to return to UL in 2001 to study for my PhD and to work in the newly built Mathematics Learning Centre, the first in Ireland. This centre was, and continues to be, a respite for students who have to study mathematics but perhaps do not particularly want to study mathematics, or for whom mathematics can be a source of great anxiety. It was such a rewarding job. Counselling was as valuable a skill as the ability to communicate mathematics. I got to see the sacrifices mature students in particular made to go to UL to complete their education. I knew the names of their children before long, such was the frequency of visits. I was so proud to be part of such a trailblazing institution that was putting students' needs at the centre. To be able to relieve that anxiety and help students to progress was an incredible feeling. The 'teaching maths for free' feeling was ever-present.

While the Mathematics Learning Centre is still very near to my heart and I continue in the role of academic director, I moved into mathematics teacher education in 2008. Again, my mentor John taught me the ropes before handing over to me when he retired. I am now in the position of helping to prepare and educate future generations of mathematics teachers.

I believe that a mathematics teacher is a very powerful person, someone students will remember throughout their lives. I want to be involved in the education of mathematics teachers who will graduate from UL and be remembered by their students in a positive light only. I believe in the power of inspiring students the way I was inspired, that saying the right thing at the right moment may set in motion great things.

Olivia Fitzmaurice is a Cavan girl living in Kerry, mum to two beautiful daughters. Loves walking, the beach, true-crime podcasts, wine, coffee, family and friends – not necessarily in that order.

DREAMS ARE THE SEEDS
OF NEW BEGINNINGS

Paddy Meskell

W hen I was growing up on the banks of the Shannon in Castleconnell, the Irish republic was less than half a century old and
was still trying to get on its feet. Whatever limited success it
was having was happening in Dublin, a day's hitchhiking east from County
Limerick. Horizons were narrow, expectations were low, and we considered
ourselves lucky to have access to third-level education.

Into this world came Ed Walsh and the dreams of a handful of dedicated
people to bring a top-class institution to Limerick, challenging the entrenched
interests of the existing order to shatter their ideas of what was possible. When
these visionaries declared their intent to build a four-year institution in Castletroy,
a NIHE that would confer honours degrees, have an international focus and

draw on an American university model, the powers-that-be were arrayed against them. Apparently, the establishment of a new university so far from the traditional model and centres of academia was beyond their comprehension. But a different spirit prevailed at Plassey. The sparkle of that spirit is even more evident today, fifty years later: NIHE, together with the National College of Physical Education (NCPE), seized the opportunity it was afforded and has grown into the University of Limerick.

And what of the initial student body? There were 114 of us pioneers in the class that entered NIHE in September 1972, about 100 of whom are still with us; another fifty or so students had entered the PE College that was co-located on the Plassey grounds. We studied Business, European Studies, Engineering, Materials Science and Administrative Systems, and had all our classes in Plassey House for the first two years.

We hung out at The Hurlers (the pub, not the bus stop). We competed with other Irish universities in several sports, from hurling to football to soccer and rugby. When we graduated, we went on to take terrific jobs at organisations like Analog Devices, the European Union, the government of Ireland. Several of us founded companies that still thrive today. I became a manager at the Electricity Supply Board and went on to be an entrepreneur and a businessman in America, and a promoter of contemporary Irish art and artists.

The close bonds that sustain this community were forged in the pioneering, pathfinding experiences we students, faculty and staff shared with the community in Limerick city and county. We developed a flinty chip on our shoulder, we gloried in our upstart reputation, our 'us against them' mentality. We had a sense of purpose and pride that we were building the foundations and culture for the first new third-level institution in Ireland since independence.

We had this sense, sometimes vague, that we were a special and unique band, selected and entrusted with this huge responsibility and carrying the outsized expectations of our families and communities. With that feeling comes a sense of possibility, of opportunity, of importance.

And we dreamed. Whether or not dreams become reality is not important.

What is important is that we dream. That we can dream, that we did dream, that we set free our shackled imaginations to envisage a life beyond the hedges and ditches of our farms, beyond the gritty alleys and small streets of our towns and cities, beyond the low grey horizon to someplace beyond. And better. And unknown.

As Ireland began to widen her horizons from the narrow focus on the land across the Irish Sea to Europe, America and the rest of the world, NIHE began to force a shift in the centuries-old definition and concept of education, from being a mechanism of control and obedience to education as a force for exploration and freedom. We, the founding students began to see our lives, not bound or straitjacketed by current realities, but fuelled by the possibilities and pathways that being NIHE students opened up for us.

And we began to find our voices, expressed through our protests, through our growing sense of justice and power in our collective strength. The sound of one's own voice can be frightening when first it's heard. But on the streets and in the classroom, we were encouraged to question, to challenge, to form our own views and ways of interpreting the world and to express them loudly and with conviction.

On the playing fields, we took on the giants of UCD, Queens and UCC, with their thousands of students and vast resources. With our bare numbers and borrowed gear, we marvelled at how a 5–0 thrashing could be transformed into a significant victory – after a few pints. And how a magnificent 0–0 result – 'they never scored!' – achieved the mythic status of the Siege of Limerick. Goliath may not have noticed, but we had just felled him. This raggedy band of players masked our intimidation by bringing our flint and steel and braggadocio to the playing fields. Later in the evening, lubricated by copious pints and stoked by packets of Major cigarettes – where did we get the money? – our renditions of 'By the Rivers of Babylon' and 'Sloop John B' in three-part harmony brought the house down.

Imagine, then, the comedown as we prepared to graduate in 1975–76, and the new government decided UL was not qualified to grant four-year honours

degrees, insisting instead that NIHE be forcefully integrated into the existing university system as a college of the National University of Ireland, rather than being recognised as a world-class third-level institution.

Undaunted, we marched in Limerick, we marched to the Dáil, we marched down into the belly of the beast at UCC and sat in. We protested, we wrote letters, we obstructed, we demanded, we went on strike and refused to go to class. We developed a warrior mentality, fighting against a stovepipe hierarchy, calcified thinking and resistance to change. And as we sang and marched and sat and drank and speechified our way through our four years, we came to admire and respect each other's courage, resilience and tenacity. We came to rely on each other and support one another.

Fifty years later, we met for our regular weekend in west Clare to reminisce, to exaggerate our adversities and mythologise our battles and victories, to share the stories of our lives and loves and wins and losses. We told and retold our old stories, holding close in our hearts and memories those who weren't there to tell theirs. Once again, the guitars came out, and the strains of Simon and Garfunkel and other 1960s and 1970s favourites wafted through the air. What a time it was.

As we once again raised the chorus of 'American Pie' to the rafters, in the dark corner of a pub in Lahinch, we had not stopped dreaming. Dreams are the seeds of beginnings. Beginnings can happen at any time in our lives. The late poet Brendan Kennelly insisted that 'we forever begin'. It is difficult to recognise a beginning in the moment of its birth. It is only from a distance, by looking back that we can identify beginnings in our lives. We can marvel at what we have begun. The dream lives on!

Those of us in the pub that night decided it was time now to pass along the dream to others who will transform the university over the next half-century. We agreed to create a Founding Class of 1972 Endowment Fund to provide scholarships in perpetuity for needy students. The endowment will be announced during the UL fiftieth anniversary celebrations. We hope they kick ass.

Lovers of the arts, in particular Irish literature and poetry, Paddy and Darlene Meskell support the Meskell UL-Fifty Poet in Residence position at UL Creative Writing.

ROOTS AND WINGS: UL'S ART COLLECTIONS

Yvonne Davis

P ublic art fosters community spirit and identity, commemorates history, symbolises growth and gives a sense of belonging. It plays a part in our evolving culture and our collective memory. It enhances our environment, transforms our landscape and chronicles our journey. Most importantly, it is designed to inspire and represent who we are, is inclusive and is available 24/7.

From humble beginnings, in an exceptional setting and with verve and exuberance, the founding executive of the NIHE, Limerick, prepared to create an environment not only of educational excellence but also of cultural vitality. The manifestation of this in real terms was a college that supported arts and culture as a dimension of everyday life for students, staff and the wider community.

Even before NIHE opened its doors to 114 students in 1972, it already held the primary object that would become the foundation of the University of Limerick art collection. That artefact of note is the lion's head fountain, which is now at the front entrance of Plassey House. It was brought from Pompeii by the Maunsell family after the excavations of 1763, most likely by Thomas Maunsell, who had served in India under Robert Clive (1725–74) at the Battle of Plassey in 1757. Maunsell purchased land near the River Shannon in the townland of Shreelane and renamed the estate 'Plassey' after the battle that had brought him such good fortune. And so it came about that, after many iterations of family homes, mills and garden markets, Plassey became the nucleus of the fledgling university.

The National Self-Portrait Collection of Ireland, one of the early collections curated at the college, was the brainchild of Dr Thomas Ryan, past president of the Royal Hibernian Academy (RHA) and Dr Edward Walsh, Founding President of UL. The collection has grown to include 500 artists – historic and modern – from the original fifteen artworks purchased from the journalist and collector Dr John Kneafsey. The collection has flourished in recent decades; it now includes works ranging from traditional media to the most innovative practices, and it continues to diversify. Later on, under the guidance of its president, James Nolan, RHA, the Water Colour Society of Ireland (a direct descendant of the Irish Amateur Drawing Society) selected the University of Limerick to become the permanent home of its members' work.

The university's desire to cultivate its art collections has always been greatly enabled by generous donations, gifts and loans from civic-minded artists, individuals, architects and collectors. Exceptional eighteenth-century and nineteenth-century paintings, gifted by the Armitage de Wilton family, grace the East Room of Plassey House, while the first-floor gallery houses the remarkable collection of Irish art on loan from the Irish American Cultural Institute (IACI). This collection is part of a greater collection comprising 400 artworks donated by Helen Hooker O'Malley to the IACI in honour of her late husband Ernie O'Malley. In addition, demonstrating her total immersion in and commitment to art and cultural life in Ireland, Helen donated forty of her sculpted busts to the collection.

The goal of having an arts collection at the University of Limerick was to form a historical and contemporary record of national and international visual culture that would provide the campus community with an inspirational academic and cultural resource. This is particularly evident in the outdoor sculptures spread across UL's vast 368-acre campus. These public sculptures are a physical embodiment of the ethos and character of the environment in which they live.

There is a quote from Johann Wolfgang von Goethe that always strikes me when walking through the campus: 'There are only two lasting bequests we can hope to give our children ... roots and wings.' I see that quote visualised in Tom Fitzgerald's 'Leaf Litany'. Installed in 1998, the sculpture at the Glucksman Library Plaza replaced a large beech tree that could not be saved when the library was being constructed. Resonating with the many trees in the vicinity, the piece is shaped from a tracery of intertwined bronze leaves and branches. At eight metres tall and topped by a canopy three metres in diameter, 'Leaf Litany' sways slightly in the wind. Around the perimeter of the pool and fountain are embedded bronze symbols of alchemy, astrology and old chemistry representing earth, air, fire, water, silver, copper and lead – references to the evolution of scientific knowledge from its early beginnings to the present day and the role of education in harnessing potential.

Even before you enter the campus, you will see, from quite a distance away, two thirty-five-metre timber flagpoles inspired by ship masts. Made from Columbian pine (Douglas fir) by Spencer Thetis Wharf of the Isle of Wight, and staked on plinths of Luget stone, the flagpoles signal the intent of the young institution to gather and inspire the next generation as it sets out on its journey to change the world. While flagpoles are often a symbol of tradition and steadfastness, the ever-changing pennants capture the university's commitment to providing as diverse and inclusive an experience as possible to all who embark on that journey.

Another site-specific sculpture, 'Geometric Forms' by Alexandra Wejchert,

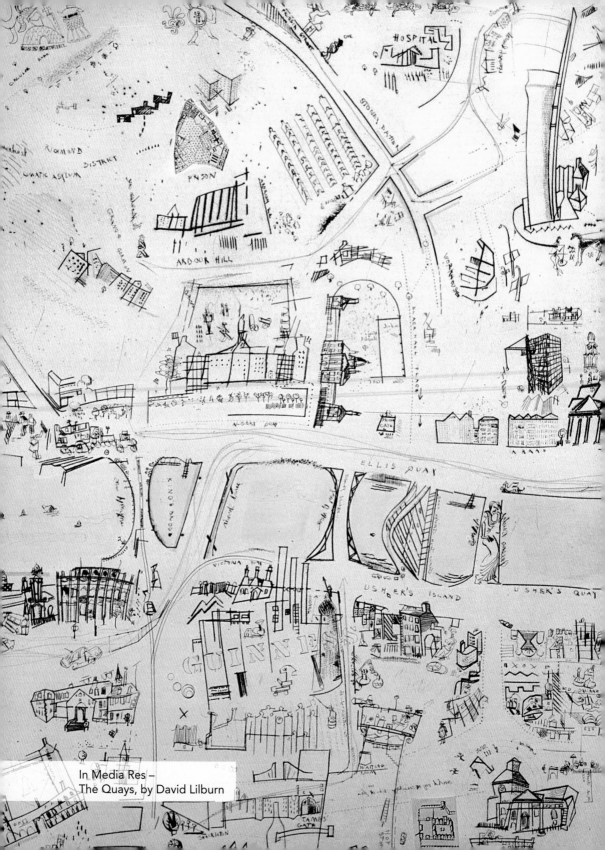

In Media Res –
The Quays, by David Lilburn

stands seven metres high on a 4.5-metre equilateral triangle outside the Robert Schuman Building. The work is constructed of polished stainless steel and comprises six identical semi-crescent elements connected at the centre. The curved fins on the main plate both reinforce the piece and add decoration. Positioned on the paved pedestrian way on the axis of the building and the ornamental pools, 'Geometric Forms' provides a pivotal point in space that binds together all the architectural and landscape elements of this part of the campus. In her own words, the artist 'wanted the sculpture to express strength and energy, its dynamic shape gripping the earth and reaching toward the infinite, the future'. The clear geometrical patterns seemed to Wejchert to be an appropriate expression of technology, science and the logic of scholarly minds, while the flow of the curving details reflects the infinite variety of thought and the restlessness of the human spirit.

The most recent addition to the outdoor sculptures, 'Niche' by Orla de Brí, stands at the School of Medicine Plaza on the North Campus. Nestled beside the copse of oak trees adjacent to the building, the piece is made of corten steel and bronze. Stretching over eight metres in height with four-metre-wide outstretched arms, the figure reflects on the 'self' – the 'student' – balancing on a point of change, choosing to grow, finding their niche in life through education, knowledge and insight, while the branches symbolise an opportunity, the future, the potential yet to be realised.

While the University of Limerick is celebrating fifty years of existence, the river, the grounds, the arboretum and the riparian woodlands have for hundreds of years beautified the area which the campus now occupies. The university's natural amenities provide us with as much ongoing benefit as the artworks that are widely dispersed throughout the grounds. Art is symbiotic, and our relationship with it is individual, formed by our lived experiences. Our unique interpretations can and will develop and change in a place where dialogue and engagement are highly valued.

My journey with the university's art collections has had many significant highlights, and not a day goes by when I do not see something anew or through a different lens. With over 2,400 artworks on campus, there is a constant shift in works that bubble to the surface, such as Mainie Jellett's extraordinary abstract works that obscure, extract and rotate the subject; Jack B. Yeats's paintings of his beloved Irish landscapes in bold and vibrant primary colours; Eric O'Donnell's 'Should they accidently fall', an illuminated glass artwork made from eighty recycled Heineken bottles; Amanda Coogan's 'Medea', a photographic still from the National Self-Portrait Collection of Ireland; Desmond Kinney's masterful mosaics – 'Sionna', 'Sweeney Astray' and 'Silver Apples'; the extraordinary collection of Molas tapestries from the San Blas Islands; and Hokusai's 'View of Mount Fuji'. I could go on and on.

On a final note, when I see students pose at graduation with their contemplative friend Brown Thomas (Antony Gormley's 'Together and Apart') or say, 'I'll meet you at the Chequer Board' (Sean Scully's 'Wall of Light'), it's evident to me that the visual arts have helped foster that special campus community spirit, shaped the students' experiences at UL and created memories they will carry with them long after they leave.

Yvonne Davis is Curator of Visual Arts at UL and in that role has organised many exhibitions and other events for our community.

ACHELOUS

Donal Ryan

I'm up on eighty now by all accounts so it must be twenty-odd years since I did a bit of building work for a man in Nenagh called Dessie Treacy. He was some man to tell a story. I often used to tip into town on a Saturday afternoon and before I went near pub or bookies I'd call in to Dessie's workshop where he had plant for hire and I'd sit in behind the counter with him and his young sons and he'd tell story after story. Some men will corner you and try their damnedest to tell you every single thing that ever happened to them in their life and you'd sooner cut off your own ears with a rusty blade than listen to them, but men like Dessie are like a kind of a channel, a conduit for all the wit and fascination beneath the firmament, and listening to them is like being weightless, painless, invisible almost; you needn't do a thing but sit still and be transported.

Dessie told me one Saturday morning about something that happened him
one time when he was out on Lough Derg fishing for pike. He was having
a good day, drawing them from the water nearly at will. Dessie had a way of
reading the mood of the water, of judging the flow and ripple of it, the spread
and density of the clouds of insects along the foreshore, the smell of the lifting
outshore breeze, the skim of mist along the surface of the water in the rising
day, that allowed him to position himself in a spot where he'd be able to whisper
the fish into his boat with hardly a need for a rod. He could sense through the
wood of the floor of his boat the motion of the shoals, feel on his hands and
face the dipping and the rising of his prey.

Anyway, on this particular day, Dessie had a boat nearly capsizing with pike,
long, razor-toothed devils of things, fish that could bite a man's arm off. A pike
will eat anything, and therefore is not considered good eating, but Dessie had
the knack of filleting and salting and buttering them into wondrousness, and
he had an empty chest freezer he intended to stock for the winter from the
bounty of the lake. Just as he was thinking of heading ashore his line tautened
and he drew and reeled but it wouldn't come, only strained his rod nearly to
breaking and pulled him along against his locked oars, and he knew he had
a big one, a king, an apex hunter trapped by another, and he was in a battle,
suddenly, so he planted his feet wide and braced his shoulders for the struggle.
A shadow fell across his boat then, and he wouldn't even have looked up if it
wasn't for the smell that rose with the falling light, an alien odour yet strangely
familiar, of ferment and mineral and the foul sweetness of decay, and he set
his rod and turned around, and filling the sky behind him was a long-necked,
wide-snouted thing, rising up and up from the dark water, green-black and
scaled and yellow-eyed, and in the centre of the yellow were two black slits, and
the apparition opened its great jaw and Dessie was looking into the deepest
depths of his own nightmares, into the fanged and fork-tongued maw of death.

He knew in that moment that the monster was warning him that he'd
taken too much from the water. That the creature straining at his line was to
be released. He turned away from the beast and back to his line and he took

his knife and cut it, and the sun shone again on his skin, and the warmth of the day returned, but the smell of death remained, and when a pike maybe five feet in length broke the water an oar's length from his side he screamed so loud he was hoarse for days. The pike broke again, nearer him, and lifted itself up from the water so that it was leaning into the timber of his stern, almost flat onto his quarterknee, and Dessie could see that his line was trailing from the pike's great mouth, and inside it was the lure he'd fashioned from a copper spoon to the shape of a baby trout, and the hook attached to it was fast inside its flesh. It rolled its eyes balefully at him, and Dessie without thinking leaned across and reached into the pike's open mouth. He dislodged his hook and his copper lure, and the sun flashed white in the pike's dark eye before he flopped back into the bottomless water of the centre of the lake.

I never met that monster myself, but then again I was never much of a fisherman. I dreamt of it, though, and I watched always when I rowed out from the headlands into the open water for its shadow, and tested the breeze for its smell, and once or twice or maybe a handful of times I sensed its presence near me, watching, and I knew it possessed the sum of all knowledge of me and of all men, of the doings and undoing of the world.

Multiple award-winning novelist and short-story writer, Donal Ryan, is a lecturer in Creative Writing at UL. In 2022 he became the first Irish winner of France's Prix Jean Monnet.

EXTRACT FROM 'SKELLBOYS'

Aoife O'Sullivan

For the end of the year, the DJ Society in UL decided that they were going to host a rave at a secret location to celebrate. It was an excellent fix to a crappy situation. There was no way we'd get away with a gaff party now, and these lads knew how to throw a proper session. They'd done it before during normal times and not got caught, so they decided with the state of the way things were, and cases going down at last, now would be the perfect time to throw one. It was quite tricky to get to the location. I don't want to give anything away, but you have to cross what's known as the Bottomless Bridge.

On a good day, you could easily swing across the iron bars of the Bottomless Bridge. It had diagonal poles crossing left and right, but the only problem is that the gaps between the bars on the floor were quite far apart, so you had to be tactical with how you swung across. This was twice as hard when you were full of drink, vision blurred by the phone torches illuminating the darkness around us. There seemed to be an endless stream of people heading off into the woodland ahead and there was a low hum of voices that acted as our guiding light. Aimee, the mad beour, flew across the bridge in front of me, to my great surprise. Sive, the lightweight, needed a bit more help.

'Hold onto me, I'll pull you over,' I said, breathlessly.

She caught my hand and grunted.

'Don't look down,' I said, while looking straight down at the water below us.

'I looked down! I looked down!' She began to quiver.

'We're nearly there look, just two more big steps and we're there!'

With a deep breath and a death grip on my hand, she made it over the second last part of the bridge, and then the last part.

Aimee came over immediately and caught her in a hug.

'Woo! Now let's go dancing!'

We walked through the shaded woods and then out into a farmer's field where we strode through the long grass while narrowly avoiding cow dung. Once off the bridge we could hear the thump of the music almost instantly. A shiver went down my spine and goosebumps started to scale their way up my arms. I had given my jumper to Sive because I had already begun to sweat profusely. I don't know if it was from nerves or excitement or both. Everyone we passed was smiling, and I smiled back at them. Our smiles turned into shock when we got to our venue.

In a little hollow, in the shade of two large oak trees sat the decks, where two of the lads from the DJ Society were playing back-to-back under a mini gazebo. There were fairy lights weaved between what seemed like every branch on the trees, and there were coloured lights behind the decks lighting up the whole hollow in red, blue, yellow, and then green.

'This is serious,' I shouted.

'Aw, what!' coming up from behind me was Tayto and he swung his arm around me and planted a wet kiss on my cheek, 'How're you, pal!'

He was on a lovely one.

'Good man, where did you disappear to?'

'Aw man, I was talking to Cory from the DJ Society, he said he'll go back-to-back with me later on if I want to give it a go!'

'Serious!'

'I said no, though. I'm not good enough yet,' he continued, to my surprise, 'but I said I'd a mate who was better that would give it a go.'

'Oh yeah, who?'

'I'm on about you, ya slow yoke.'

I was shocked. Tayto had actually put me forward to go on the decks at this rave. The both of us had always hopped up on the decks at our own house parties and at Dicey's and all, but never in front of a crowd we didn't know.

'Aw what, that's dacent.'

The night was off to an excellent start, even if it was only our own gang of friends at the beginning. The tunes were absolutely pounding. I had no idea how they got all the gear into the middle of this farmer's field, as well as the lights and a generator to power the whole thing, but it was not a time for questions. The night seemed to go in slow motion, which was perfect, because none of us wanted it to end. I hadn't felt like this since my last night in Dolan's during rag week. Word quickly got around UL and Limerick city that the rave was on. At around 3 a.m., there must've been at least 150 people there, ripping up the little hollow with their leather lace-up boots and Nike runners. The long grass we were standing on was completely flat from everyone dancing on it, and the muck had become completely exposed. There was plastic bale-wrap spread out for everyone to sit on when they needed to take a breather, and to be fair to the lads, there were people going around with bin bags for cans and bottles of water for those who needed it. It was some set up. I stayed with Sive for the whole night. It felt like we were at a festival together. I saw people that I hadn't seen all year. I even ran into some of my old housemates from first year and caught up with them. It was like the whole place had mutually decided they were going to be in the form of their lives. Everyone was on a love buzz.

It got to 4 a.m. and I looked at my phone in awe, 'How have the shades not come yet, this is unreal!'

Sive clicked the button of my phone off, 'Put that thing away and just enjoy it!'

I laughed and twirled Sive around as we danced, and then she did the same to me.

Then I got a tap on the back, 'Jamesy, ju wanna hop on so for a while.'

Cory Martin beckoned me to follow him up on the decks. He was a mad-looking feen with a mullet gone so long it curled at the back, and seven piercings between his nose and his ears. His fringe was so high up on his forehead I was convinced he had cut it himself. He was wearing a vintage Adidas raincoat that had a noticeably weird smell off it. It wasn't long before he was sweating so much he had thrown his top off into the ditch behind him. I hopped on the decks eagerly. I was so full of drink I didn't have time to be nervous. The music was already at a high bpm, and I searched through Cory's tunes to keep it going.

'Aboi, Jamesy,' Tayto roared, causing a tidal wave of appreciation for me from the crowd.

I played for a good forty-five minutes with Cory's help, and then as the morning started to slightly peep through, I decided I had to finish with something classic. *Blue Monday* by New Order caught my eye, and without doing anything fancy I threw it on and left the decks to jump into the crowd with my friends. Everyone went nuts. People weren't singing the lyrics, they were shouting them. Normality. It felt so wrong to enjoy it, but it was beyond our human nature not to. I threw Sive up on my shoulders and Tayto did the same with Aimee. Tayto shook his can of Bud and sprayed it all over us and everyone else around us. It started pissing rain, soaking us to the bones, but nothing mattered. There isn't a form of currency on Earth that is worth these memories, but fuck it, I could use a loan of a quid for the bus home.

Aoife O'Sullivan, Bachelor of Arts in English and Irish (2022), wrote 'Skellboys', a piece of fiction set around UL during the Covid-19 pandemic, as her Final Year Project.

WALKING PAST THE RUSTY MAN: NURSING AND MIDWIFERY

John McCarthy, Aifric Devane, Sandra Healy and Shelagh Meskell

Not quite a mature student, I chose at twenty-one years of age to study nursing, selecting the University of Limerick as my place of study. I chose UL as I knew people who had studied there previously, the prospectus was varied, and a trip to Limerick for a walk through the campus reinforced my judgement – the place just felt right. Walking past the Rusty Man, I decided that UL was the ideal college for me to embark on my nursing studies.

In the late summer of 2002, I began my UL journey, joining the first cohort of BSc Nursing (General) students on a four-year adventure that would see me graduate as a degree-holding registered general nurse in the summer of 2006. Equipped with the necessary clinical skills that my UL education provided me with, along with an analytical, critical-thinking, holistic approach to nursing care, I began working as a staff nurse on a medical ward within the University Hospital Limerick (UHL) group.

The four years spent in UL, learning, living and maturing, helped me to become a nurse who could fully appreciate the honour of caring for people at their most vulnerable, supporting them throughout their recovery, all the while working as part of a wider team aiming to provide an impeccable service to those who need it.

As my career progressed, and the years moved forward, I returned to UL in 2014, to complete a single module on Infection Prevention and Control in Healthcare. It had been eight years since I had graduated from UL as a registered nurse. Walking through the campus, again greeting the Rusty Man, I thought to myself that I had aged, but not him. He looked as young as ever and seemed to welcome me back to his campus. On completion of this module, I once again departed UL, this time with a keen interest in the area of infection control nursing.

The next few years saw me taking on managerial roles as a senior staff nurse, part of service provision within the hospital. I frequently acted as nurse-in-charge, and as managerial positions became available in 2015, I successfully interviewed for, and accepted, the post of Clinical Nurse Manager II on a medical ward. Now a manager, with years of clinical practice behind me, I felt the need to bolster my new position with a managerial course. An easy decision to make by now, I found myself returning to UL in autumn 2017 to study Health Services Management in the Kemmy Business School.

For me, this experience was both fulfilling and empowering. Empowering, as I could now appreciate with deeper understanding the decisions made within the hospital group and the health services in general. I took back to my workplace greater awareness and understanding that enabled me to become a better manager, of workloads, people and myself. Again, thank you, UL.

Completing the first year in Kemmy allowed me to continue my managerial studies by enrolling in a BA in Management Practice in autumn 2018. At this stage, I considered myself a seasoned learner and very much part of the UL family. After completing this BSc, I do not know why, but I thought this might be the last time I would enrol as a student of UL. As I left the campus and walked towards the car park, I gave the bronze man an appreciative nod and smiled goodbye to the flagpoles. My career continued, and I took on the role of managing a larger ward specialising in the care of patients with renal conditions. I also became involved in various successful service-enhancing initiatives undertaken within the hospital group.

The autumn of 2019 saw me receiving emergency medical care. A life-changing but enhancing event in many respects. I was cared for in UHL by nursing and medical colleagues, many of whom were fellow graduates of UL; my extended family, if you will. The care I received was exceptional, and a testament to the holistic, person-centred education that UL provides its graduates, and the care that UHL provides to its service users.

I have long since returned to UHL, now as a CNM II in Infection Prevention and Control. Captivated by the memory of waving goodbye to UL in 2019, I am once again greeted by my bronze friend after enrolling in the MSc Infection Prevention Control Leadership programme. My footsteps again join and merge with those of fellow students crossing the bridge towards the Health Sciences building. Shimmers on the water below mirror the excitement on a student's face. The excitement of a new beginning. Thank you, University of Limerick. *— John McCarthy*

In 2008 I joined the BSc Nursing (General) programme in UL as a mature student, qualifying in 2012. My first four years in UL were only the beginning that paved the way for my future career as a nurse. On qualifying, I was fortunate to be appointed as a registered general nurse working for the Alzheimer's Society; a post I held for four years. Throughout this time, I developed an empathy for and awareness of how difficult life can be living with dementia. In 2015, I completed a Postgraduate Diploma in Public Health Nursing (PHN). Over the last seven years, as a PHN, my commitment to people living with dementia has continued to grow. In 2019 I completed a UL Postgraduate Diploma in Dementia Care. Engaging with lecturers whom I had previously studied with, along with renewed opportunities to enjoy the UL campus, positively contributed to this learning experience.

In September 2020, I commenced an MSc in Advanced Practice (Nursing). This was the first year that this programme was offered in UL as part of a national consortium collaboration. At the time of writing I am now in year two of this innovative programme, advancing my practice in dementia care. This semester, as I work towards completing my MSc in 2022, I reflect with positivity on my years studying at UL. I am proud to have developed professionally and to have fuelled my compassion to improve the lives of people who live with dementia. I look forward to emerging as a Registered Advanced Nurse Practitioner in Dementia Care. — *Aifric Devane*

I am a practising midwife. I graduated from UL in 2010 with a BSc in Midwifery. I was part of the first cohort of the direct entry midwifery programme in Ireland and so did not require a nursing qualification to register as a midwife. Midwifery came to me as a somewhat unexpected career choice. An empowering homebirth experience with my youngest child prompted me to become a midwife. The experience was life-changing and I wanted to ensure that more women had access to this option of care.

Initially I worked as a hospital-based midwife, but since 2016 I have been providing a HSE homebirth service to the women in the mid-west of Ireland, and the joy and satisfaction I receive from this career is immeasurable.

My relationship with UL did not end in 2010, as I was lucky enough in 2012 to receive a scholarship to pursue a PhD while I continued working part-time as a midwife. I graduated in 2018 and I must honestly say that this period was one of the most enjoyable of my adult life. I was immersed in a topic that I was passionate about; I met many wonderful people who enriched the experience for me, and I had an opportunity to teach midwifery students, which was one of my highlights.

I hope to continue providing a homebirth service for women for many years to come and would love to see more midwives considering this as a career option. — *Sandra Healy*

After years working as a care assistant, supporting people with intellectual disabilities, I yearned to learn more and to have the opportunity to develop my skills. Becoming a nurse was always a dream, but I was nervous to take the plunge. Through encouragement and support from family and colleagues, I applied to UL, knowing that they had a renowned Nursing and Midwifery department. I was very fortunate to receive a place in the BSc Intellectual Disability Nursing Degree programme, starting on the path of becoming a nurse in 2008.

The four years went by in a flash. I absorbed all that I learned, putting theory into practice and gaining the requisite skills and knowledge through the combined university and practice placement training. After qualifying in 2012, I began my nursing career, equipped with the tools that I needed to holistically and respectfully support the individuals for whom I cared, this time as a nurse.

In 2016 I commenced my first nursing management role. The years in UL gave me the drive to further enhance my learning and skills. I continue to work, proudly, within my service, now as a Clinical Nurse Manager 2 and I have the pleasure of being involved in many wonderful things. Supporting individuals with intellectual disabilities to live fulfilled lives, integrating into the community and empowering people to achieve their hopes and dreams has been extremely rewarding. I hope to return to UL soon, to further develop my skills in the place where my career truly began. — *Shelagh Meskell*

John, Aifric, Sandra and Shelagh are graduates of UL's Department of Nursing and Midwifery.

FROM UL CONFESSIONS:
A SELECTION OF FIFTY TWEETS

The UL Confessions page was launched by an anonymous student or students in January 2020 as an online space for students to share thoughts. As such, it is a window into everyday campus life at UL. Students post through CuriousCat.qa, a service that allows users to exchange messages without being identified. Content ranges from sardonic, amorous or satirical posts to conversations about distress, anxiety and homelessness. The editors of this book have selected fifty tweets.

Just wondering does anyone know what would happen if you bring a horse to the Stables? Has anyone ever tried it? It's a question I've always wondered about.

•

To the people in Groody who were shouting around the place after 1 a.m. last night, I hope your pillows are warm on both sides tonight :))

•

I slept outside around the football fields for weeks over a semester once. Ended up financially not being able to carry on with my rent. Ashamed so never told anyone but with everything that's going on around student accommodation these days I feel as though I should.

•

RIP to the poor guy throwing up in Groody last night, I never heard sounds that scary in my life.

·

Why do all Irishmen have the same long-on-top-short-on-sides haircut? My tinder likes look like Star Wars clones.

·

Whoever was doing the 'Dory speaks whale' from Finding Nemo impression outside my window in Kilmurry ... 6/10, good effort. Maybe not at 1 a.m. next time.

·

To the guy in his car taking a deep (audible) sniff of his armpits that I made direct eye contact with, I am sorry.

·

There should be an introverts' club where introverts go to the pub and drink then talk to each other.

·

To the person in Groody who plays the drums in the middle of the night, could you just not.

·

Shoutout to the lad from Stradbally in my accommodation who was grooving to Incan music in his boxers with his door half open. Say no more.

·

Couple in the main building eating the face off each other for about 2 hours. And they said romance was dead.

·

Whoever that lovely boy was that gave me the last place on the bus so I could go to my dad's, you're a gem x

·

Hello to the cute girl reading the heavy metal book in the library café this morning and her only.

·

Did anyone see the fella getting carried out of Flannery's looking like Jesus on the cross?

•

To the people blaring Ludovico Einaudi in Oaklawns at 3 a.m., who hurt you that bad?

•

Balding society in UL. We can all meet up and support each other, talk about our feelings and the stigma around balding, and then when we are leaving we can rub our lovely shiny bald heads together in appreciation of our balding brothers.

•

The fact wearing Carlow jerseys on Valentine's Day isn't normalised baffles me.

•

I am starving for a girlfriend.

•

Sometimes I cheat on Wordle.

•

If we ever fleetingly make eye contact in the library, just know it's not an accident and I do in fact love you.

•

As the girl who was struggling coming into college thank you so much to the person who wanted to reach out and help me privately in dms, you are truly a good human.

•

Why are we getting 7000 emails a day?

•

To the guy looking up My Little Pony in computer lab marry me please. No need to be ashamed.

•

Any time I miss my mammy I go into the library café for food because the ladies in there are just so lovely to you.

•

College is so lonely, all my mates in relationships, my roommates never leave their rooms, literally twiddling my thumbs on the couch every night wishing I'd someone to talk to even.

•

Didn't write acknowledgments in my FYP but if I had to I would've given a big shout out to Lidl energy drinks.

•

Sometimes I wonder what it would be like to attend college and the only stress is being able to do college work instead of working a part-time job to pay for all my expenses like college fees, accommodation and cost of living. Some people really don't know how lucky they have it.

•

My housemate keeps feeding my hamster rice. How do I get him to stop?

•

Convinced that there's something in the water up in Mayo as all the boys are actually beautiful.

•

How long does it normally take for a supervisor to accept or decline your FYP proposal?

•

Housemate had a shower at 4 a.m. Is she potentially a sociopath?

•

Not sure there's anything sexier than a Tipp lad #weakattheknees

•

To the girl in the bathroom singing It's a New Dawn It's Going to be a Great Day, can I just say I love your energy.

•

Went home with a lad and there was no hurleys in the porch, walked straight out again.

•

Best place to get a nose piercing in Limerick?

•

Was in College Court last night with techno DJ and a fella ating two bowls of porridge in middle of rave.

•

If I'm around some friends and they start making plans for going out or whatever, I never say anything. I'm too scared to invite myself in case I'm imposing on them so I can only ever go if I'm invited, like a vampire. As a result I haven't been out once this semester.

•

Saw a lad going around a house party in Elm with a measuring tape, measuring people's foreheads then asking some of them to leave, some ppl do be melted.

•

I don't know how to say this, but I love how our student officers are usually just normal students and actually reflect UL students. It was so different where I did my undergrad.

•

Molly's should have the music louder, I still have partial hearing left.

•

9 emails from UL in the last 4 hours. Do they ever take a day off?

•

My housemate thinks I'm weird because I eat tuna and Tayto sandwiches. Best thing ever.

•

You are weird. *[From UL Confessions administrator]*

•

Literally nobody actually likes techno. Y'all just pretend to be cool.

•

Petition to ban granola bars and really clicky mouses from the library.

•

Cork boys bring nothing but misery.

•

Is a girl having fairy lights in her room a red flag?

•

Petition to make it mandatory for all UL lads to have a pic with Brown Thomas on their tinder as a height reference photo.

•

My Twitter is logged in on my Nan's laptop just so she can read UL Confessions, the woman thinks it's great.

•

It's gotta be said, UL Confessions is the best confessions page out there. Sincerely, your friends from UCD.

SIX PHOTOGRAPHS

Sean Reidy

Image 1 (overleaf): Heron, May 2009

I first spotted this heron fishing in the stream that runs between the PESS building and the Lonsdale building. What astonished me was how many people walked blindly by, utterly unaware of its presence. Having learned that stillness gave it a cloak of invisibility, it was hiding in plain sight. It simply froze and watched whenever people passed. I took some photos of it there, but the background was cluttered. After a time, the heron flapped languidly upstream and stopped near the entrance to the Schrödinger Building. That is where I took this picture. There is wildlife all over the UL campus and the river if we only have eyes to see it and ears to listen for it. Apart from the usual small birds, it is sometimes possible to see otters, kingfishers, foxes, cormorants and pheasants on the campus. But you have to take your face out of your phone screen and really be present in your environment to win the rewards that openness to nature brings.

Image 2: Poetry Reading on the Living Bridge, November 2007
There was a small group taking part in a poetry reading on the Living Bridge on this night in November 2007. A very long exposure was needed for the picture, so people walking on the bridge were blurred. But this group, wrapped and rapt, stayed relatively still.

Image 3: Peace Procession, September 2010

In September 2010, UL students held a candlelit peace procession from the Plaza to the north campus. The students held electric candles as they walked across the bridge. A minute-long exposure created a flowing river of light.

Image 4: The Lion in Winter, December 2010

The winter of 2010 was very cold indeed. Several weeks of sustained below-zero temperatures froze lakes and created winter scenes everywhere. The campus became a winter scene. If memory serves me correctly, an elderly motorist got confused one evening and tried to turn his car on one of the snow-covered fountain ponds in front of the Schuman Building, thinking it was a car park. Predictably, that didn't end well. This lion's head fountain outside Plassey House froze into stillness, while the cobwebs, normally invisible, were covered in frost.

Image 5: A Flurry of Frost, December 2010
Two days before Christmas, the wintry campus was hushed and almost empty.
At first glance this looks like falling snow, but these were wind-blown flakes
of hoar frost dislodged from a tree near the Glucksman Library.

Image 6: Through the Trees

I'm not sure when this was taken, but it is clearly a summer image. The Rusty Man is framed by the leaves of the Plaza trees. He has suffered many indignities over the years: the graduation selfies, the woolly caps, the sunglasses and the placards hung around his neck. And he will endure many more. But on this day, he basked in summer sunshine.

Sean Reidy is a retired staff member of UL, currently having a blast exploring Europe in his motorhome with his faithful dog.

Steeplechase runner and Olympian
Michelle Finn at UL

AN tOILEÁNACH

Neasa Fahy-O'Donnell

Growing up on Oileán Acla (Achill Island), sport, for me, was initially water-based. I soon progressed into athletics (cross-country), winning various underage county and national titles at the National Community Games. At secondary school, also in Achill, PE was only outdoors, a choice of basketball, camogie or, when it rained, Latin. I kid you not!

From the age of fourteen I dreamt of being a PE teacher or working in sport. My parents, both teachers, were influential, as was a chance trip, in my Leaving Certificate year, to Limerick's Thomond College of Education (TCE). Four wonderful, enlightening years later, I was one of twenty-three proud graduates of the class of 1993. In TCE, I made friends for life ('the Mollies'), all keen sports heads, but, for me, involvement in student sports clubs was a critical element of my settling into a whole new phase in my young student life.

Our TCE lecturers had a huge impact on my love and appreciation for physical activity and sport. No wonder, given the tutelage of teaching legends such as P.J. Smith (RIP), Dave Weldrick (RIP), Anne Sweeney (RIP) and Pat Duffy (RIP), along with Joanne Moles, Teresa Leahy and Carmel Vekins, to name a few standouts. Teacher training and sport became more than physically doing, it was now about discipline, philosophy, psychology and overall well-being, while moulding teachers of the future. My curiosity for the world of sport was ignited.

I left TCE a more rounded person, but two years into my teaching career a call from Carmel Vekins, head of Physical Education and Sports Sciences, offered me an opportunity to return to my alma mater. I couldn't resist. Now married to my Donegal husband, Paddy O'Donnell, also a UL employee, whom I met through GAA in TCE/UL, living in Limerick and starting a family, this was a no-brainer.

I loved working in PESS, but again in the summer of 1999 my career took another unexpected turn, when an opportunity came across my desk to join the Sport and Recreation Department. Interviewed by Dave Mahedy, Head of Sport, the late Dermot Foley (ULHR) and Jacinta O'Brien (PESS), I was catapulted into the job of my dreams. My passion for sport and recreation was now truly blazing and within a few short months I knew this was to be my future. All this time since first coming to UL, I reflect on the most amazing years of my life.

What I love most about working with students is their ability to keep me feeling young and challenged. While I may be ageing, the students, with whom we have the pleasure of working remain young (average age of twenty-two). Their enthusiasm and desire to learn and excel is infectious and knows no bounds. As a student, I trained on the infamous field known as 'The Mud Patch', where now stands the UL Sport Arena, the foundations of which I also walked. I looked on in awe and pride as sport facilities grew and expanded over the next twenty-plus years. I was part of this dream and vision, my reality being my ability with my fabulous sports colleagues to help students bring their sporting dreams to life.

We have witnessed years of sweat and tears, early morning sessions to late nights returning from competition, and, somewhere in between, time for the studies. Students pushing themselves to their limits, to achieve their best, at all levels of sport, from the absolute beginner to world-class Olympic and Paralympic athletes. The knowledge, appreciation, respect and encouragement that an Intervarsity title might be the highest aspiration and fulfilment for one student, while the ability to podium on the international stage is the end goal for another, has kept me inspired. Twenty-plus years of supporting, steering and guiding student athletes to achieve and reach their best potential, the highs of wins to the lows of losses. We have lived this with them; the many turns and twists along their sporting journey but knowing never to give up. This is what the UL dream is about.

I am privileged that my work in sport brought me to the world stage as Chef d'Équipe/Head of Delegation to Team Ireland at the World University Games Taiwan in 2017 and Deputy Head (Gwangju 2015, Kazan 2013 and Shenzhen 2011), leading Irish athletes competing against current and future world champions and Olympians. From flying the UL flag to raising the Irish tricolour, sport keeps us hungry and alive. Students come and go, some you will never forget, but we remain true to our cause. Being part of this UL family is very, very special. The years pass and the next cohort of dreamers rolls in, and so the story and the evolution of sport at UL continues. UL dreams can and do become a reality. Twenty-seven years (51,840 hours!) believing and working with amazing students and colleagues has taught me this, as I continue to live my UL dream.

Neasa Fahy-O'Donnell is UL Senior Executive Sports Manager and Chair of Third Level High Performance for Student Sport Ireland.

IT'S THE KIND OF PLACE
A BAND DREAMS OF

Noel Hogan
(in conversation with Eoin Devereux)

When the band [The Cranberries] started out, we used to rehearse in a small space called the Storeroom in Xeric Studios on Edward Street, Limerick. All the other, more established Limerick bands at the time told us that The Stables was *the* place to play in order to gain experience and that the guy to approach was Ber Angley. By lucky coincidence, Ber lived not too far from our family home. I plucked up the courage and asked him if he might allow us to play in The Stables. I gave him a copy of our first demo tape and he must have liked what he heard.

When we did play there, it was very nerve-racking for all of us. This stood in contrast to our earliest shows in Limerick City where the audiences were

THEM
NOTHING LEFT (MIKE)
HOW
A TOSA
SERIOUS
PUT ME DOWN
PAT. SCEN.
REASON
UNCERT.
LINGER
I STILL DO
12
STORY
DREAMS

University of Limerick
Students Union Entertainments

THE CRANBERRIES
THEATRE ROYAL
FRI 17 DEC

DOORS OPEN 11 P.M.

Price incl VAT: 7.00
No: 74   R.O.A.R.

made up of our friends, which was a kind of safety net.

At our first UL gigs we were very inexperienced. We'd rather look at Fergal Lawler's drumkit than face the audience. The Stables gigs were different, too, in the sense that we were performing in front of an audience who were unfamiliar with our songs. One thing I do remember about The Stables was that the stage was really high. It meant that, when you were playing, you were looking at the top of everyone's heads. As a young band starting out, it was difficult because, owing to our ages, we had no transport. Sometimes our parents drove us to The Stables gigs with our equipment in the back seat of their cars. My father was a baker, and he was also a part-time bread delivery man. His van was used a few times to transport The Cranberries to UL.

The Stables gigs were a great place to test out new material. Our songs 'Dreams' and 'Linger' would have featured in those early gigs. Ber Angley was great. He really looked after us. Even though we were 'nobodies', he treated us really well. From there, Ber helped us further by putting us on a tour of the Irish college circuit and while we played relatively few gigs in Ireland this experience helped us hone our craft. College circuits are really important for young bands. Our big break in the USA was as a result of playing the college circuit and being played on college radio. Building on our Stables shows, we began to play bigger gigs, at the 1990 UL rag week, in UL-organised gigs in the Parkway and in the Jetland on the Ennis Road, where we signed our record deal with Island. At that point we had begun to have a good following locally and in the Limerick college scene. There was a bidding war going on to sign The Cranberries. That UL gig was the biggest gig we had ever played. We weren't the headline act, we played for forty minutes, and it went really well. It was at that show that The Cranberries decided to sign with Island Records.

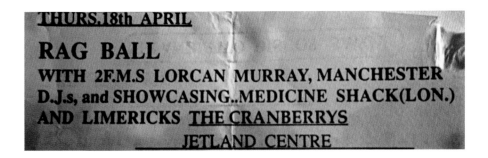

THURS.18th APRIL
RAG BALL
WITH 2F.M.S LORCAN MURRAY, MANCHESTER D.J.s, and SHOWCASING..MEDICINE SHACK(LON.) AND LIMERICKS THE CRANBERRYS
JETLAND CENTRE

When our debut album *Everybody Else Is Doing It, So Why Can't We?* eventually broke in the USA, it was Ber Angley and the ULSU who organised our sell-out homecoming show in the Theatre Royal, Limerick in December 1993. UL Campus TV filmed that gig, and many years later we used some of the footage when we re-issued 'Zombie'. In 2016 we returned to UL, to the ICO Building, to rehearse and record our album *Something Else*. I had previously worked with Ken Rice of the ICO on one of my solo recording projects. Having played an MTV 'Unplugged' Session in the past, The Cranberries were keen to reimagine some of our songs and use string arrangements. The UL campus and the ICO building was a really relaxed place to work in. Dolores was staying in Limerick city, and as the rest of us live locally, it was an ideal place to work and record. It was the first and only time we recorded a full album in Limerick. It was the start of a longer relationship between the band and the ICO. We went on to use the ICO space to rehearse before we went on tour. Dolores loved working there. She was living on Henry Street at that time and she'd walk to UL by the riverbank.

We were left alone to do our work. It's the kind of place a band dreams of. It's big and spacious and The Cranberries were able to do their pre-production work there. The ICO was so accommodating to us. I have one fond memory of some fans arriving at the back door and Dolores invited them in to say hello. Working in UL at the ICO building was a really productive time for the band. I have kept up my connection with UL and was delighted to collaborate with the Centre for Popular Music and Popular Culture on their conference and book on Joy Division. We were honoured to be invited back to UL to receive honorary doctorates. Being honoured in this way was special for all of us and our families. It was a joyous but bittersweet day, as we all keenly felt Dolores's absence. Little did we think in 1990 when we first trod the boards in The Stables that we would be invited back to UL decades later to have the band's global achievements honoured.

Renowned guitarist, songwriter and producer, Grammy-nominated Dr Noel Hogan taught himself guitar at the age of seventeen. He became a founding member and main composer with The Cranberries.

PLACES MATTER

Sindy Joyce

I was the first Traveller in Ireland to graduate with a PhD. In one way, it's exciting to come this far for my people, but for decades upon decades, from the foundation of the state, we have been excluded from everything, including the arts. We are a nomadic people; the name Traveller was put onto us as a community, but we are not called Travellers in our own language. In our own language we are actually called Mincéirí, which I suppose not many people know. And because of our nomadic ways, people put the name Traveller on us.

They didn't know what to make of us. With the foundation of the state here, we were a separate group. The national identity was really important for Ireland, to give a new image to the world after years of British occupation. We can see how Irish people were stereotyped across the globe, and Ireland wanted to move away from this stereotype and give itself a new modern image, with a national identity, with its own culture and its own language and its own traditional ways. And in doing that, Ireland forgot about us as a community and left us to the side, as if we weren't included.

We can see that through the history books. There's no mention of us in any history documents, any history books. It's as if we have just been wiped off the face of Irish society as a people. And it's an important step for the Arts Council to come up with this [Equality, Human Rights and Diversity] policy, which is a really bold statement. However, we can also look at the seventieth year of the UN Declaration of Human Rights: that was a bold statement seventy years ago. Policies can be bold; they can seem like they are a utopia. But they are not.

If you have the right people working with the right frame of mind to push an agenda forward, that's what's needed in all parts of society. For my people, we are very much involved in the arts, but we are not seen in the arts scene. A big part of our tradition is art: it's arts and crafts, singing, dancing, handcrafts, the wagons we built that we used to live in. When I look at the arts in Ireland, I can see some things that would be seen as Irish tradition, we can see our connection within some of these arts, but it's not acknowledged.

There's lots of cultural appropriation as well. There are lots of things that were made by us as a people, which are in museums and other places, but we are not acknowledged as the artists. For example, I was walking through one museum a couple of years ago. We stopped at an exhibition; it was a homestead exhibition, so it was looking at Ireland in the 1940s and 1950s and how people lived. And in one little corner there was an item that was made by a tinker. A lot of tinsmiths in my community were called tinkers because of the tin-smithing, it was a lamp. That was the Traveller section.

It just gave me that feeling of here we go again. Totally excluded. With one word written up.

So, people coming in and looking aren't learning about our culture, our identity and our traditions, or learning who we are. All people are seeing is the negative stereotypes that are portrayed across the media and people need to see more of the positive things within our community through the arts. I would

like to just ask you all, whatever line of work that you are in, to make sure that you are looking at all parts of society, and that you are not leaving anybody out. It's all okay having these fancy policies, beautiful policies; what good are they if they are on the shelf? They are on the shelf for years, gathering dust.

Last year the Minister for Housing came on national TV and he was looking for recommendations on how to fix the Traveller housing crisis. And I was basically roaring at the television saying, 'How many more recommendations do you need?'

It's similar in all sectors of society. Listen to the people that are giving you the recommendations. As a people we have, so many times over the past thirty years. Sometimes I feel like a broken record, giving advice, giving recommendations, giving key points. People have to realise, come together and start to debate things, and within the debate you have to make people feel a little uncomfortable in order for them to reflect on themselves and their own attitudes and ideas and prejudice about everything in society. And including about themselves, they need to reflect on themselves.

Once you reflect on yourself, and you get an idea of who you are as a person, you can begin to reflect on society and how society works, and how it works better when everybody is included and nobody is excluded.

Even if we look at design of buildings. Some buildings are totally inaccessible for some groups in society. Even for me, a university campus ten years ago would have been totally inaccessible. I was overwhelmed my first time going in there, this was a new space. I always get tired of things being overwhelming or feeling a place is not for you. Or you feel like you are an imposter, you feel like you don't belong. Or I feel that I'm always the only Traveller in the room, the only Traveller on a panel. You look around and you say, 'Where are my people?' And you look at everybody in society then, and you ask, why is that?

It's because we haven't thought about including everybody in society. We have thought about including people who look like us, who talk like us, who act like us, who have the same aspirations and ideas as us, but we don't look at people who are different. People who would have different ideas that would

push and drive things forward. People who have new ideas and ideas that need to be recognised. And these ideas need to be recognised as part of a collective and not as an individual piece of work, it's a collective.

Irish society thirty years ago was totally different. It was totally different for the general society, but for us it was even more different, because we were more isolated and more marginalised, our traditions, our nomadic ways, our arts and crafts. Everything had been decimated. Our culture had been basically criminalised, because it became illegal for us to travel around Ireland and we were forced into these, what they call halting sites.

The first halting site was built in 1968. We can see how the government actually went abroad and looked at how other countries were dealing with 'difficult groups of people' and got ideas from that. This came back, and this is how halting sites were thought up as a plan. They are concrete jungles; they are not something we asked for as a people. We didn't ask to be forced into these halting sites, marginalised and separated from general society and isolated from everybody else. Places matter. Places do matter.

Because when you are in a place in society, not only in the physical sense, but where you are isolated from everything and everybody, you are isolated from services, you're isolated from people. You're isolated from communities. And if you are isolated from communities, how can you be part of community? Places do matter.

My doctoral research was on young Mincéirí between the ages of fourteen and twenty-one; it was that age where it was really important for them to figure out their identity and who they were and to realise what place they had in society. I did lots of qualitative work, focus groups and walking around the city to different places with them. And the thing that struck me was when we were walking around were the comments they made; they were asking, do you see any representation of us in the city? Where are we? Between the buildings, the architects, the art, the graffiti, all the things that are displayed, the cultural identity that is displayed, but yet none of that represented my people, and for the young people it really traumatised them. It gives them a sense that we're not wanted here in our own town, in our own city, in our own country.

I would have hope and aspirations. And hopefully in between five and ten years' time we'll see a difference, and we'll see many more people included in the arts in Ireland.

From an address to the Arts Council Conference 'Building Inclusion in the Arts' (2019). Dr Joyce is an indigenous Mincéir, a human rights defender, sociologist, UL lecturer and member of President Higgins's Council of State.

ONLY TIME WILL TELL

Jennifer McMahon

Leaving Certificate 1996. English. My favourite subject. I stare at the essay titles in front of me. One of them stands out: 'Only Time Will Tell'. In a single moment everything I've been holding back comes flooding onto the page. I write about pregnancy, about the loneliness of becoming a solo parent, about frustration with adults who don't listen or don't want to hear, about the decision to have and keep a baby in the face of misplaced shame and stigma. Mostly I write about feeling scared and small but needing to be fearless and as big as the world. I write about a birth, a baby in arms, and I ask if the decision was the right one. There's just one answer to this and of course it's how my essay finishes. Only time will tell.

I will never know what the examiner made of the essay. Did they consider it a work of fiction or did the strength of emotion conveyed persuade them that I'd

been telling my own story, writing with the conviction of personal experience? Regardless, it was a pivotal moment for me. No room for regrets. Everything made sense. My baby and I embarked on our adventure together.

There were interesting years to come. I worked as a musician, writing and singing in one of Ireland's first electronic bands, held down many part-time jobs and eventually found my way back to education and the joy of books. I graduated with a doctorate in psychology. But where to next? The University of Limerick had always loomed large on the Limerick landscape. For a Limerick native it might seem like it should have been nearer and more accessible than other universities, but that's not always the case. Expectations, economics, social capital and support can smooth the pathways to university no matter where it's located. As for me, working in UL felt for a long time like an elusive dream. But in the end, my path led me here, a confluence of hard work, passion and very good luck.

Nowadays my head is still stuck in texts (and baby is all grown up), but I've largely swapped Brontë and Yeats for authors in peer-reviewed journals. I work to promote youth well-being and mental health, an area my younger self could have provided great insight into, which is why I particularly value the voice of young people in my research. I bring my love of music and creative arts to my academic work too, exploring them as a means of enhancing youth well-being. Limerick at my core, the university is a gateway to a wildly rich and diverse community that I have a passion to serve and to act as an advocate for its positive growth.

After almost a decade here I have found ways to carve out my academic life while also nurturing my creative self. This hasn't always been easy. I'm consistently inspired by others around me who have transcended the ordinary, untethered to a version of themselves through their creative endeavours. And so I've navigated the space, pouring my emotional self into songwriting and finding those extraordinary moments connecting with musicians and audiences through music.

With one foot firmly on UL soil and the other in the stars, there is still much to do and dream of. And with no time to look back yet, and much time still ahead, I can't help but feel that, so far, my younger self would give the seal of approval.

Dr Jennifer McMahon is a psychologist whose research interests span the areas of disability and mental health. She is the founder and director of the i-TEACH (Teaching for Inclusion) research lab.

FIND THE RIVER

Melissa Mora Hidalgo

My heart fluttered as the train pulled into Colbert Station. My chest swelled and my eyes grew misty as I watched the clouds sweep in over the hilly green landscape dotted with cows and castles. Through train windows, Ireland looked as familiar and like-home to me as the foothills, canyons and freeways of LA. And though we were coming from Cork via Dublin, places I knew from previous visits and many train rides before, the land around Limerick was different. This part of Ireland tugged at me, reminding me that I once lived here, too.

My friend texted and told me to look for a red Škoda parked across from the station. But I didn't need to because I saw him first in his impeccable silver quiff and black Morrissey T-shirt, waiting for us, cross-armed with a smile, under a blue sunny-cloudy Munster sky.

My face broke into a big smile as I held my arms out, not caring that my runaway luggage ambled towards Parnell Street. We hugged real big on the plaza in front of the train station, my partner a loving witness to a happy reunion between friends, colleagues and UL family.

'Welcome home,' my friend said.

And I was.

My first formal connection with UL was in 2015. I was invited to give a keynote at the *Songs of Social Protest* conference. I returned for six months between 2016 and 2017 as a Fulbright Scholar. It was my first time living abroad, and I was 5,000 miles and an ocean away, far from my partner, family and home in greater East LA. I landed at UL in late August 2016, hauling my life in an overstuffed backpack, two giant suitcases and a carry-on tote bag filled with whatever last-minute items had seemed important enough to take.

The man with the impeccable quiff collected me from the train station, welcoming me to Limerick, then took me for my first bites to Castletroy's Delish café and dropped me off at my Kilmurry Village apartment. My new home would be steps away from the room my partner and I stayed in the year before when I delivered the keynote, so it was all very familiar, and it felt good.

I remembered other places at UL from last time that would ground me as I found my bearings: the Munster Rugby training grounds and facilities; the library and lecture halls with Brown Thomas in front; The Scholars' Club and the bus stops in front of The Stables; the Irish World Academy and Pavilion restaurant across the Living Bridge over the mighty River Shannon.

Even so, landing in Limerick in 2016 was bittersweet: for all of the familiarity and like-home moments so far away from home, I couldn't shake an unsettling feeling. My beloved aunt was dying of cancer back home, my grandmother was suffering from Alzheimer's disease, and a Republican candidate for US president was driving a national campaign fuelled by violent racist, misogynist, homophobic, anti-immigrant, anti-Mexican, 'America First' red-state rhetoric.

That election marked the halfway point of my stay in Ireland. I was both anxious to go back home to fight Trumpism but also determined to make

Limerick feel like home, because for so long, I had dreamed of exactly the thing I was doing: getting paid to live, read, write and travel in Ireland. I didn't want to waste the precious few months I still had at UL. I had great friends and colleagues, a beautiful campus and a few thousand euro in my Irish bank account. I had work to do and a home to make.

On campus, I wrote at The Scholars', the Pavilion, my desk in the Foundation Building, and the Sports Club. On weekends, I walked to the markets and the off-licence carrying back groceries and cans of Guinness, four bags at a time, slowly filling my kitchen with stuff I'd buy at home: pasta, fresh veggies, oatmeal, milk, butter and olive oil, wine, cheese, breads, teas and sweets. I fell into a regular routine of porridge for breakfast, lunch on campus or at a pub, and pasta or a sandwich at home for dinner.

When I missed my ultimate morning comfort food of breakfast burritos, I'd walk to Lidl or SuperValu for flour 'wraps' (because there were no tortillas yet in Limerick), eggs, cheese, bacon, potatoes for filling, tomatoes, garlic, scallions and 'coriander', AKA cilantro, for a fresh *pico de gallo*. For a lunchtime bean burrito, I'd mash black beans with a little cheese that I'd wrap up and warm on the griddle pan I used as a *comal*.

Apart from occasional trips to Galway, Cork, Dublin and Waterford, I found myself wanting to stay in Limerick, to get to know the area better. When I wasn't busy working on campus or writing in the library, I went to Hook and Ladder for coffee and pastries, and Lana for Asian noodles. I took the Green Bus to Ennis and Adare for day trips, walked up the Dublin Road to Annacotty for a view of the river falls. I took the bus to the city centre and walked around end-

lessly, the lovely River Shannon my guide to Dolan's for music and pints, or to Clancy's Strand for the best views of Limerick City across the bridge. I went to Thomond Park for Munster Rugby matches, got my hair cut at DaVinci's on Thomas Street, bought a winter coat at Debenhams, and hung out at Flannery's on Shannon Street before taking the 304 bus back home.

For dinner sometimes, when I grew tired of pasta and bean burritos, I'd go to Kilmurry Lodge for a burger and pint, or stay in and order delivery from the Indian place around the corner. At night, after I couldn't read or write anymore, I'd camp out on the little sofa in my apartment and watch re-runs of *The Simpsons* and *Narcos* on Netflix, or gameshows we didn't get in the United States.

At bedtime, the Shannon healed my heart and filled my soul. She kept me company everywhere I went in Limerick and led me back home to 4 Kilmurry Village, after long days out. Every night, I listened to her flow outside my window, her waters hushing me to sleep as I sent prayers with her out to the ocean and all the way home.

• • •

It took five years and a Lesbian Lives Conference in Cork to draw me back to Ireland. I was excited about Cork and Dublin, but I was giddy about my 'homecoming' to Limerick. I couldn't wait to see and visit my old stomping grounds, couldn't wait for the views of King John's Castle and the Shannon. I wanted to see the new Boojum eatery and the Treaty City Brewery. I wanted to visit Kilmurry Village, listen to the river rush by, and have a pint at The Scholars'. Above all, I wanted to see my beloved 'homie-lads', my three friends and colleagues who became my UL family.

As we rounded the bend and slowly pulled into Colbert, I felt a warm wave of emotion come over me. The scenery, the signage, the on-board announcement spoken in Irish then English, the familiar sensory experiences of riding on Iarnród Éireann that brought sweet memories of living in Limerick to the surface. I looked out onto the Irish landscape, a grin growing on my face as I spotted things I recognised, like the rolling hills of County Clare in the distance or the shopping mall I'd pass on the bus from UL to the city.

I looked over at my partner, and I flushed with pride and love. The train stopped, the butterflies started. A smile was plastered on my face, my neck wrapped with a red Munster rugby scarf under a flat 'paddy cap' I'd bought in Ennis.

'You're home, dear,' said my partner, reaching over to hold my hand.

And I was.

Dr Melissa Mora Hidalgo is from greater East Los Angeles. She finished her 2016 book, Mozlandia: Morrissey Fans in the Borderlands, *on a Fulbright Fellowship at UL.*

UL TO ME WAS A PLAYGROUND

Paul O'Connell

(in conversation with Joseph O'Connor)

I was coming out to UL for swimming when I was four and five years of age. UL, to me, was a playground.

It was a place where there were loads of places to do sport. My mum and dad didn't go to university, but they both worked in De Beers out in Shannon. So we would have been doing every single sport under the sun. I was in Seal Swimming Club and one of our training sessions would have been here in UL. NIHE at the time.

It was a thirty-three-metre pool. It was unusual; I know people will remember it. You couldn't dive in at the shallow end, your hands would scrape the floor. I can remember vividly, there was a beautiful diving pit next to it and we used to be able to nip in and out of there. It had big glass windows on one side that

went out almost to the reception area of the swimming pool, so you could look out at the people there and they could look in at you. It was a really cool feature.

Swimming was the start of it, but then, on a Saturday, we'd use the gyms. The older kids would be lifting weights and, as it was called back then, doing callisthenics. Then the odd time Mam would drop us down and we'd play squash. This is when we would have been eight, nine, ten.

My first fish, I would have caught on the black bridge here. All along the riverbank we used to go running. I did soccer camp here when I was seven or eight. I always felt UL was open and it was the place you did your sports. It was brilliant. We would have been very independent. Mam would drop us in to UL. She could trust us; she'd go to work, I'd go fishing for the day. I'd be ten or eleven then.

On the far side of the river, when there was no building whatsoever over there, I camped over there with my friends. It was magical. Amazing. The river here is beautiful.

I took up rugby at sixteen, then I got picked for the Irish Schools. Rugby wasn't particularly my thing, but I thought, 'I mightn't be too bad at this.' And Munster were beginning to come good. So I joined the gym here, about seventeen, and started doing my weights here. And literally, until I retired as a professional rugby player at the age of thirty-five, I would have been going in and out to UL all the time. So, it's a second home in one way.

I used to live five minutes away. We moved not too long ago, and I'm two minutes away now. I do get recognised the odd time, very occasionally on a night out I might get asked for a selfie, but people know Limerick is your home, they don't annoy you. My kids go to school locally. Castletroy and the area around here is a very cool place to grow up. You've walking, running, cycling, camogie, Gaelic football, golf.

I studied here. I didn't finish my degree [in computer engineering]. Student life was amazing, I became great friends with a group of Kilkenny lads who lived in College Court. For them it was party time, not so much at all for me, I was dipping in and out of it, living on their coat-tails a bit. Rugby was becoming ever more serious for me. I'd drive over and see them but then maybe leave early because I'd training the next morning. But I really regret that I didn't finish the course. I convinced myself it would have been a distraction when really it wouldn't have. It would have been a good thing to take my mind off the game. A lot of the players now, they have their heads screwed on, they're all doing courses and degrees, but I didn't finish mine.

To be a professional sportsperson in the city where you grew up in is absolutely amazing. But it did mean I didn't finish out my degree or, say, go on a

J1 to America, or do a year in Australia or take a job in London. By the time I retired from rugby, I was supposed to go and play in Toulon in the south of France for a couple of years, but I got injured, so that didn't happen. I might go back to study again someday, who knows. If I did, I'd say it might be psychology or philosophy. I've gone full circle now, in that I think English is probably the most important subject in school. Being able to express yourself. Even now, when I'm coaching, I try to get a lot of my coaching instruction down into a one-pager.

Sports is forever changing. And rugby has its challenges, around injuries, and then it's a tricky game to coach, it's fifteen a side. Anyone can rock up and play a game of five-a-side soccer, but you can't play five-a-side rugby. Some positions are very specific. But I think everyone in Limerick played or followed or watched rugby, and I don't think that's the case in the rest of the country. There's great fun in Limerick around the joking and the slagging between clubs. Limerick is a sporting city. And look at the facilities in UL, the amount of 4G surfaces, it's amazing. We'd come down here regularly as a family, get out of the car with frisbees, hurleys, soccer balls, rugby balls.

The most important time to learn rugby is when you're young and small; you learn to tackle before anyone is too fast or too big. A small player can take down a big player provided you know how to tackle properly. That's what I love seeing. And a rugby team is very highly interdependent.

I think the green jersey is the most important jersey in world rugby, for the reason that we play as one island. You've British people playing for Ireland. I think it's a real privilege if you're from the south to play with someone from the north. It's something I've thought about a lot since I retired. Sometimes I wish we'd made more of it. It's an unbelievable achievement, what we've done in rugby in Ireland. You can be Irish and British and European or whatever else you are, you don't have to be exclusively, vehemently one thing.

In terms of one thing I'd like to change about UL, the connection to the city would be a big thing for me. UL should be such a big part of the city. Our amazing location is the reason why we have these great sports facilities, but the university should be the heart of the city. I feel UL is disconnected from the city, and the city has suffered because of it. If that connection was there, the city would be younger and more vibrant, and the city centre would be more attractive. Maybe a better travel corridor that connects the city and the university. The university owns a very significant property in the city now. But we can't half do that. It needs to be a monumental job. Limerick people had to agitate for this university to come here. It's always been like that in Limerick. We've always had to battle. And it continues to be like that. We should be a really exciting, edgy university city, a fun destination to live, to work and play. I'd hate if it took another fifty years.

Paul O'Connell is internationally acclaimed as an icon of sport. He captained Munster, Ireland and the British and Irish Lions, and is Ireland's third most-capped player of all time.

A CONVERSATION WITH DENISE CHAILA

Caoimhe Gaffney

S tanding out from the crowd and breaking norms can be difficult, especially for women. Women tend to undervalue their strengths and over-apologise for their weaknesses. However, Zambian-Irish rapper and spoken-word poet Denise Chaila is ready to fight against these stereotypes and break with tradition.

Denise arrived in Ireland from her hometown of Lusaka, Zambia, when she was just eight years old. In 2012, she moved to Limerick, a city she describes as 'a city of poetry'. It was here that Denise found her true love of words, using her heritage and identity to weave her thoughts and opinions into lyrics and music. She began by writing poetry, giving the regulars at the White House Poets reading event on O'Connell Street a very different performance than they were used to.

When I moved here, I went to the White House, the pub, as a spoken word poet. Those guys were doing Seamus Heaney and I was doing Nikki Giovanni, and I was the only Black woman there. I was younger than everyone by about thirty years, but it worked. I loved it. I went there, and it was like, all these old guys with Guinness. I'd go after school with my friends or my dad and I'd stand in the corner with like some tea and I'd wait for my turn and I'd be there trembling, hands shaking. I'd go up and I'd take the mic and everyone else had manuscripts that they had printed off and I'd have my phone. I'd be up there for like five, seven minutes, just reading out these really long, existential poems about Blackness or sexuality or womanhood or trauma. Someone else would come up afterwards and be like, 'This is a poem that I wrote about birds after the birth of my second child'. I thought wow, we are very different!

Denise was transformed by musicians such as Lauryn Hill, Missy Elliot and Saul Williams. Although music was her passion, Denise was devoted to her faith and joined a Brazilian church group in Limerick. It was here she met God Knows and MuRli, members of Limerick hip-hop group, Rusangano Family. Their friendship blossomed into a deep spiritual connection with one another, eventually leading to the creation of Narolane Records.

After featuring on the Rusangano Family's track 'Isn't Dinner Nice?', Denise jumped headfirst into hip-hop. Hip-hop in Ireland was still viewed as something strange and taboo, but she was ready to challenge these stereotypes and she claimed hip-hop as her own.

Hip-hop is a vehicle for the imagination, the voices and the revolution of black bodies and white spaces. It means and represents a historical movement, feeding off of the civil rights movement into a new generation of people who were trying to identify themselves in a world who told them who they were was wrong. Hip-hop artists are rattling the cages of a machine that has spent their whole lives telling them who they were and what they were allowed to do. Through this music, as a vehicle for dreams, they have an authority to speak to heteronormativity and class, and space, and to take up space that few other places afford them to do. Hip-hop moves and operates as a body that creates space for everybody on the margins to almost have the same claim to authority as our institutions, through performance.

Hip-hop is a feeling, an energy, a permission to say that all of these scripts, for what it means to be a woman, or queer, or a Christian, or Irish, or Black, don't quite fit me, and it feels weird. Hip-hop is the place where I see people actively taking charge of their definition and saying that's not who I am and I'm going to tell you who I am. In Limerick for example, when you look at the people who are involved in hip-hop, they are really distinct to me and my community of brothers, because we all have something to say.

Chaila was suddenly faced with the challenge of being a woman in a mainly male-dominated workforce. She was determined to make a space for women and prove her gender meant nothing when it came to her talent.

I have a real issue with the term 'female rap' actually. I think that it is a reductive, essentialist term that reduces me to my biology because I'm a woman, not a female. The subgenre, it creates a distinction, a segregation between who's allowed to make real rap you know? Because rap is what men do, and female rap is what women do. As a female rapper, it's not an all-access pass. It says that you can be accepted, but it's always going to be on someone else's terms. I don't see that in any other space, in any other industry where we talk about female doctors, female architects or female jockeys to the same degree.

Denise also expressed concern with the lack of acceptance surrounding hip-hop music and its artists in Ireland. Live hip-hop was rarely played on Irish television shows and there was little visibility for its musicians. Although hip-hop took over the UK's music scene many years ago, Ireland was slow to follow.

There's no blueprint but unfortunately in Ireland, to even talk about rap music is somehow something shocking and new for people. Add the element of femininity onto it and you end up running into people's shame complex of sex and sexuality, because, whether you like it or not, as a woman involved in rap you are coded as sexual before a word even leaves your mouth. That's because Black people are coded as sexual and rap is a Black art-form. This is the sort of thing that we're all fighting against, why everyone's liberation is so important to hold at the same time.

After getting a taste for what being a rapper was really like, Denise was unstoppable.

My career kind of took off at the start of this pandemic. I keep on wondering what my demographic is. Is it like teenagers? Is it twenty-five-to-thirty-year-olds? My demographic is babies who like to spell words and people who like morals and change. People who want to change the world, and babies who are here for a bop. It's a really beautiful thing to sort of be a part of a world and a space and a time where I can be complicated in that way.

After a stream of national television and radio appearances, Denise quickly became one of the country's most prolific young artists, dubbed on Twitter as 'a national treasure'. However, her position came at a cost. She was faced with hordes of online racial abuse, eventually resulting in her asking RTÉ to stop tagging her on social media platforms.

> I think most institutions are extremely irresponsible with how they handle black bodies in the media. We're still in the place America was, pre-Trump, where we take these people's threats and comments as a joke, and I think that because of that apathy and passiveness, we are heading towards some extreme, extreme national trauma because these things bubble to the surface. We are not fine until I have the opportunity to essentially be an artist without making activism a necessary part of my work. That's already indicative of a poison, you know?

Although Denise lived in Dublin when she first came to Ireland, she has now truly made Limerick her home. In August 2020, she was awarded Limerick Person of the Month, a prize that is very close to her heart.

> It's an award the citizens of Limerick choose to give to someone. I represented Limerick very consciously, saying, 'This is my city' and unless I take a stand for something that I love, no one is going to hand me permission to just belong to somewhere. So, I said, 'This is my city, this is my city, this is my city' for years, and my city kind of said, 'This is my girl.'

Caoimhe Gaffney is a UL BA graduate in Sociology and Politics with International Relations. Her Final Year Project for the L-Pop Research Project focused on women and hip-hop in Limerick. Denise Chaila studied English, Sociology and Politics with International Relations at UL.

'TO THE APPARENT DELIGHT OF THE STUDENT POPULATION': FROM A REPORT ON THE LIVING BRIDGE

Conor Lavery and Keith Brownlie

The UL Living Bridge is a pedestrian bridge designed by Wilkinson-Eyre Architects and Arup. The bridge was a key component of the University of Limerick's expansion from its established campus on the south bank of the Shannon to its new annexe on the opposing bank in County Clare. The north bank was opened up for development in 2004 by the 150-metre long 'salmon-tail' road bridge 420 metres further upstream, also by Arup with Murray O'Laoire Architects.

The new bridge was placed at the heart of the campus to provide a direct pedestrian route between academic faculties and student residences, spanning across the river, its banks and floodplains. The two sides of the university are both physically and visually separated by the Shannon and the riparian landscape of the river corridor. This ecologically sensitive and internationally important environment is a 'hidden' delight, and the design responds to this essential quality of the site with a structure that is threaded through the landscape and invites users to engage with their surroundings.

The bridge presents a deliberately modest visual statement, spanning at relatively low level in an organic and iterative relationship with the site.

Alignment

The bridge takes a 350-metre-long curved alignment on a 300-metre radius in six equal spans, each comprising an independent bridge structure crossing between table-like pier sections. The most southerly span crosses the pedestrian riverside walk and its environs. The central spans cross a secondary parallel waterway on the south side and the river itself, whilst the most northerly span crosses the boggy floodplain. Each bridge deck waists from seven metres width at the pier to four metres at centre span. The curved edge profile is countered by a tangential reverse-curve on the pier sections, creating a continuous 'pulsating' geometry that binds the component parts into a coherent whole.

The Shannon's flow at this point is considerably reduced by a hydro-electric diversion upstream, creating a wide shallow waterway fragmented by islands of woodland growth in the channel. The horizontal alignment is arranged such that each river pier is coincident with one of the wooded islands. The pier footings provide upstream extensions of the existing islands, and act as cutwaters to protect against erosion and movement of these transient landscape features. From the riverbanks and the campus, the bridge is seen not as a continuum, but as a series of short bridges spanning between tree clusters. For the pedestrian, the islands are effectively stepping-stones, connected with spans in the manner of an ancient clapper bridge. From each end the curving deck is seen to 'disappear' into the landscape, without sight of the opposing end, and the bridge user is temporarily enclosed within the natural environment of the river corridor. Views of the destination unfold as the journey across the bridge progresses.

A key component of the university's brief was to provide a facility for enjoyment of the river landscape, as well as a linear connection between the two halves of the campus. To reinforce this situation the deck is separated into two delineated zones. On the outer edge of the curved deck a 2,560-millimetre-wide continuous aluminium walkway provides a sinuous pedestrian 'fast lane'. The remainder of the deck, surfaced in a bonded aggregate finish, varies in width from a narrow strip at each centre span to a wide gathering space at pier locations. These gathering spaces feature seating and shelter against the backdrop of the tree canopy, to provide students with an off-campus location for informal meeting and study.

Spans

The bridge comprises a string of six independent 44-metre spans with nominal 8-metre-long pier sections. The primary load-bearing structure of the spans is located below the deck in the form of a pair of edge cable-trusses, providing a restrained aesthetic and allowing unobstructed views from the deck. The shallow water means that the river is not navigable and experiences limited level flooding, which allows the use of this relatively uncommon structural type, aligned to achieve a 4.2-metre clearance over the river at mid-spans.

A 50-millimetre diameter stainless-steel handrail follows the sinuous line of the deck edge and a tensioned stainless-steel cable mesh provides transparent infill. The deck structure comprises a longitudinal fabricated steel beam inset from and integral to the cable-truss top chord.

Piers

The five pier locations have been designed to minimise the impact at ground and river level. They feature a steel deck supported on a four-legged steel 'tetrapod' in an inverted pyramidal form. On the western edge of the pier decks, a 'vertically' cantilevered glass screen is inclined at the same angle as the adjacent parapet. The screen frames the tree canopy beyond and harbours an integral bench assembly facing into the deck. A second bench construction in the centre of the deck acts as a cutwater for pedestrians, separating the continuous walkway from the refuge, and allowing face-to-face seated gatherings.

Lighting

The lighting strategy is to reinforce the pulsating geometry with linear and repetitive sources on the spans and to intensify and diversify the lighting at the bridge ends and piers. A variety of sources are employed, incorporated into the superstructure and deck furniture in a discreet manner. The approaches to the bridge feature glass lens pavement lights which are floodlit from beneath with strong colour to define a legible threshold to the crossing.

Dynamic Characteristics

The slender lightweight form of each span presented a number of challenges to overcome in respect to the dynamic performance of the deck. Tension bars beneath the walkway surface were adopted to greatly increase the lateral stiffness of the deck, increasing the fundamental frequency of horizontal vibration. It was, however, a design objective that bridge users should experience some vertical acceleration of the deck. The vertical dynamic performance of the spans was assessed against the criteria in BS 5400 Part 2 and response factors were calculated using an Oasys GSA footfall analysis. The analysis indicated that the first two modes of vibration were in the vertical plane, having a frequency of 1.3Hz and 1.5Hz respectively. As the second vertical mode of frequency is close to typical walking frequencies, it was anticipated that the bridge user would experience a small degree of acceleration. In use, the bridge experiences single person vertical excitation, to the apparent delight of the student population.

Construction

The bridge is situated within a special area of conservation which contains protected spawning grounds for a number of fish species and supports protected woodland. Consequently, all in-river works were confined to an environmental window of two and a half months for piling, pilecap construction and the erection of temporary works. During this window a temporary bridge running parallel to the line of the permanent structure was founded on stone gabions placed directly on top of the riverbed. Steelwork fabrication was undertaken by Eiffel and their subcontractor Viry in the east of France and transported in modules to Limerick. The five northernmost spans were then assembled in a compound on the Clare side, and the remaining span constructed on the more constrained south. The northern spans were driven into position across the temporary bridge using a self-propelled multi-axle vehicle transporter unit positioned beneath the ends of each span. A tandem crane lift was undertaken to position each 100-tonne span on top of the tetrapod supports. Following erection of the spans, the remaining finishes were applied to the bridge deck, working from the permanent walkway. The bridge was opened quietly in November 2007 and quickly began to operate as intended, carrying a significant footfall but also, critically, being used as a destination for social interaction within the university campus.

Keith Brownlie, RIBA, RIAS, FRSA, is a British architect with extensive experience in the design of major infrastructure and urban design projects, especially bridges. Conor Lavery, associate director with Arup, led the structural engineering of the Living Bridge.

THE NEURODIVERSE COLLEGE EXPERIENCE

Charlie Mullowney

I t's week six of my second year in college; I'm sitting in an exam centre. There's me, one other student and a supervisor. That supervisor just happens to be one of my lecturers.

It's okay. No need to panic. Deep breath, you've got this. Or at least, this is what I tell myself. In reality, I am filled with anxiety.

The material is extremely abstract and difficult to learn, never mind remember. Add to that my inability to regurgitate what I've been taught. The result, I keep all of my emotions in, until they finally flood out of me. After trying to keep myself calm and collected for the first hour or so, I finally give up involuntarily. Fortunately, the other student has left at this stage; otherwise, the embarrassment, like my anxiety, would have escalated tenfold. Suddenly

I'm bursting into floods of tears. The supervisor comes over to calm me down and reassure me. Not only have I humiliated myself in front of a lecturer, now I have to continue with this near-impossible test.

This was most certainly not one of my finest moments. I've had many struggles but also many victories. One of my proudest moments as a college student is becoming a 'dis'ability advocate. I'm fortunate to have used my academic life to shape myself into the writer and advocate that I am today. So let us start at the very beginning. In the words of the great Julie Andrews, it's 'a very good place to start'.[1]

The first piece of academic work I have written from a 'dis'ability lens is my essay on Ursula K. Le Guin's 1973 short story, 'The Ones Who Walk Away From Omelas'.[2] As part of my essay, I argued that the child in 'Omelas' is non-binary and has selective mutism. One of my main arguments is that society views the child as 'abnormal'. My argument showed that the oppression of the child by the citizens of Omelas was representative of the oppression of the 'dis'abled community by modern-day society.

In fact, this module led me to expand on Lennard J. Davis's *Enforcing Normalcy: Disability, Deafness, and the Body*.[3] My blog post discussed how what may seem to be a need to some is considered a privilege to others.[4] I talked about the societal expectations of personal independence, freedom from family, increased risk of stigma, and increased risk of vulnerability. I used Davis's binaries of 'normal' and 'abnormal' to contrast social norms with the reality for 'dis'abled young adults. I addressed the social norm of young adults moving out of home 'once they start college or reach the age of 18,' which may not be achievable for 'dis'abled young adults. This ties into the reality that many 'dis'abled young adults often rely on parents and/or guardians for financial, physical, mental and emotional support. I expressed my opinion on how societal norms cause 'dis'abled young adults to feel stigmatised by society and have a sense of internalised ableism. Finally, I explained that 'dis'abled young adults are prone to vulnerability, due to being likely to struggle to trust others to be kind and compassionate.

College helped me become the 'dis'ability activist I am today by educating me to be articulate, critical and aware of the theory that can help me make compelling arguments.

College as a 'dis'abled student can be challenging. Between getting around campus, attending lectures, and managing workload, student life is complicated, to say the least. Nevertheless, Disability Services, especially Caoilinn Shinners-Kennedy, Thomas O'Shaughnessy and Peter Dooley, helped me get through any and all difficulties I faced during my time as an undergraduate, and now they help me as a postgraduate student. As I have already shown, exams cause me extreme anxiety and stress. Disability Services have helped me with exams by appealing for me to be given alternatives to most of my exams. When these alternatives could not be provided, I was provided with a separate exam centre, extra time, spelling and grammar waivers, and a scribe.

Two of my 'dis'abilities are dyspraxia and dyslexia. My dyspraxia makes my writing illegible, even to myself. My dyslexia means I have trouble with spelling; this makes writing and doing college work more time-consuming. Thanks to Disability Services, I am also given assistive technology, which helps with these challenges.

Two exams, in particular, were panic-inducing disasters. One was a first-year exam, where the questions had the plays and themes I had revised, just not in the right order. For the second exam, I couldn't get an alternative to an exam; I would have made it to the test if my stress hadn't caused me to get the date mixed up. I almost had to do a repeat for each of these exams. Fortunately, Disability Services fought my corner throughout all three exam situations I have mentioned. Their help included contacting relevant lecturers to eventually get me an essay replacement. After weeks of correspondence between both sides, I was able to submit essays instead of having to retake the summer exams. Unfortunately, I had to do a lot of studying before I knew I could do these essays, which caused a lot of stress.

Nevertheless, completing the essays was a lot better than having to face another exam situation. For this reason, I am forever grateful for the help of

Disability Services. Caoilinn helped me with everything from time-management to workload management to assignment help, to reminding me to make time for my mental health. Caoilinn is one of the reasons I suffered college and have a job. She is not only currently my boss, but like a sister I never had.

It was an honour to have my work chosen to be presented at the All-Ireland Conference of Undergraduate Research (AICUR). As a 'dis'ability activist, I am adamant about showing that popular culture unfairly misrepresents the 'dis'ability community. My Final Year Project compared the Netflix series *Atypical* and self-representation from 'dis'ability activists Chloe Hayden and Jessica Kellgren-Fozard. Presenting my research at AICUR meant I could inform more people about the misrepresentation of autistic individuals and provide them with an authentic, first-hand experience of the neurodivergent community. Neurodiversity is an umbrella term for any neurological 'dis'ability, including autism, ADHD and dyspraxia. Neurodiversity follows the social model of 'dis'ability, which states that society's view of 'dis'abilty is what causes an individual to be seen as 'dis'abled, not the 'dis'abilty itself.

My greatest achievement to date is getting chosen for Gorm Media's series, *This is "Them"*.[5] The series spotlights the concerns and opinions of individuals from various minority groups in society. *This is "Them"* gave me the platform

to speak on issues within the autism community that need to be heard but often go unnoticed. It was an honour to work with Gorm's founder, UL PhD student Mamobo Ogoro. I am genuinely inspired by all that she is achieving, especially in terms of activism, in such a short space of time. She is definitely one of my role models in terms of people putting themselves out into the field of activism in such a public way.

Another memorable time in my life was my work placement with I Love Limerick. If I'm honest, I had the occasional stressful moment, including an eating disorder-related panic attack. But I've also had so many unique experiences, including having a casual conversation about vegan cheese with the drag queen JuJuBee, who is, to use an Irishism, 'sound' and super sweet. I also gained so many social, life and independence skills that I would not have achieved within my more academic semesters of college. Overall, college has shaped me to be the person I am today. This short memoir allows me to do what I love the most about writing, using my voice to inform and encourage others, and that alone is an honour in itself.

Notes

1   Hammerstein, Oscar and Richard Rodgers, 'Do-Re-Mi', from *The Sound of Music*, performance by Julie Andrews, 1959.

2   La Guin, Ursula, 'The Ones Who Walk Away from Omelas' (1973), pp. 1–4.

3   Davis, Lennard, 'Visualizing the Disabled Body', *Enforcing Normalcy: Disability, Deafness, and the Body* (Verso, 1995), p. 125.

4   Mullowney, Charlie, 'The Privileges of Normalcy' (2021), The Voice in the Darkness, https://thevoiceinthedarkness.home.blog/2021/02/14/the-privileges-of-normalcy/ (accessed 05 August 2022).

5   Gorm, 'Autistic Women Answer YOUR Questions | This is 'Them' | Gorm', This is "Them" (2021), www.youtube.com/watch?v=MRDawx9b63E (accessed 05 August 2022).

Charlie Mullowney is an Irish disability activist, studying for a Master's in Technical Communication and eLearning at UL. She is a member of Disability Power Ireland.

TRÍ DHÁN / THREE POEMS

Mícheál Ó hAodha

Ag an bhFronta (1916)
(Do. Pat Gallagher a fuair bás sa phuiteach - Ar dheis Dé go raibh sé – RIP)

Nuair a thost na gunnaí sa deireadh
níor dhóigh leat riamh
go raibh an bás ag déanamh oirchille
sna trinsí.

Tásc ní raibh ar a chuairt
ná a rian i súile
na mílte marbhán
ná sa bhréantas a d'fhág sé ina dhiaidh.

Má tháinig an bás in aon chor
is go fáilí a ghabh
trí na trinsí fola
is teanga
trí scáthán scoilte an mhaidneachain
is allagar scaoilte na n-éan,
an ghrian
a éiríonn fós san áit thoir.

At the Front (1916)

(For Pat Gallagher, one of the thousands who died in the mud – RIP)

When the guns finally fell silent
you wouldn't have thought that
death had ever lurked in the trenches.

There was no log of its passing
no trace in the eyes of
a thousand dead corpses
or in the stench that it left in its wake.

If death visited at all
It must have passed furtively
between the trenches
of blood and language
Between the cracked mirror of the dawn
Or the loose talk of the birds,
The sun
that still rises in the east.

Fuaim na Deoraíochta … (Mam)

Báisteach ar m'fhuinneog
Caoineadh gearr is an tost a leanann
Fuaim imeachta gan filleadh

What Emigration sounds like … (Mam)

Rain on my window
Early bird's short cry and the silence afterwards
The sound of leaving and never returning

An Nuacht ón mBaile – Nóta ó Mham
(Huddersfield, Sasana 1987)

an chuach dhílis fillte arís i mbliana
grian na maidine ar m'fhuinneog
an bháisteach sna cnoic
an ghaoth is an féar ard ag damhsa

The News from Home – A Note from Mam
(Huddersfield, England 1987)

the faithful cuckoo has returned again this year
morning sun on my window
rain in the hills
the wind and the high grass dancing

*Mícheál Ó hAodha is a poet from Galway who writes mainly in the Irish language.
He has worked in the Glucksman Library for twenty-five years.*

JIM KEMMY: IN MEMORY

President Michael D. Higgins

The year 2022 marked the twenty-fifth anniversary of the untimely passing of socialist, historian, rights advocate, Limerick man, and to so many a dear friend, full of principle and humour too, Jim Kemmy, who died at the age of just sixty-one. Throughout much of his political life, Jim was an outsider: a socialist in a politically conservative state, and a social liberal in a socially conservative city.

His death in 1997 was all the more poignant given the wave of social progress that had just begun to wash over this country in the years leading up to his passing. For example, 1993 had seen legislative bills enacted to allow for the widespread availability of contraception and the decriminalisation of homosexuality, while in 1996, the year before his death, divorce became legal. A rapidly growing economy at the time enabled some socio-economic progress, with

area-based initiatives helping to tackle disadvantage in a number of so-called poverty blackspots, including Jim's home city of Limerick. All of these changes came from the influences of the collective labour and trade union movements to which his life was dedicated.

Jim Kemmy was an optimist, an idealist who believed in the power of progressive politics to liberate people from lives being lived under exclusions and the dominating control of the Church, a state that paid scant attention to the poor and that had, in its ideology, privileged property, that had averted its gaze from the drudgery of poverty and disadvantage, and whose policies had reinforced rather than challenged inequality and colluded with the Church to maintain a society that was repressed, had eschewed solidarity, but rather expressed views that were often cruel and hostile towards those marginalised. Jim would point to the fact that, as an exception, and after a long struggle, he had been elected in Limerick, a city which he somewhat kindly had called 'not the most progressive in the world'.[1] He saw this as a source of optimism for social progressives like him.

Jim Kemmy's life is exemplary in its dignity of combining hand and brain in life and struggle. After having qualified as a stonemason in 1957, he immediately left for work in London, whereupon he was introduced to trade union activity, thus embarking on a lifetime of activism in the labour movement. During this time he developed an enduring love of reading, becoming introduced to socialist writings, and would later come home 'lugging a backbreaking suitcase full of books'[2] including the works of Marx, Engels, Connolly and Larkin. A self-taught man, having been an early school-leaver, Jim was erudite and passionate about the ideals contained in these classic texts, which formed the basis of his vision for society. It is fitting that, given its mission to integrate the economy, society and the environment to deliver a cohesive pedagogical programme, the University of Limerick has named its business school after Kemmy.

Jim's following was strong among younger and more radical members of the Irish Labour Party where he became a member in 1963. He clashed with those he saw as lacking radical instincts or cowed with excessive caution. This he saw as serving the interests of the enemies of the workers. His organising of anti-apartheid protests against the South African rugby team when fellow Labour TD for Limerick East, Stephen Coughlan, as mayor, felt obliged, because of his office, to welcome them to Limerick, divided him from some comrades, but his deep sense of social justice superseded any political or career aspirations.

His desire for separation of Church and state was a key motif of his political career. He condemned what he deemed 'extravagant' spending on the 1979 Papal visit, and he regularly turned down invitations to attend religious events, such as the consecration of Dr Jeremiah Newman as Bishop of Limerick.[3] Yet Dr Newman would, until his death, regularly contact him for disputations and discussion.

Reproductive rights would become an ongoing struggle in his political life. His heroic campaigning for contraception earned him condemnation from the pulpit on a number of occasions. Indeed, he was elected to Limerick City Council in 1974, having advocated in his election literature a social and cultural revolution to include the availability of contraceptives and the deletion of Articles Two and Three of the Constitution. He became chairman of Limerick's family planning clinic and famously responded publicly to an anti-contraception statement from Dr Newman by informing him that 'women [...] are increasingly regarding sexual intercourse as an expression of personality and a physical pleasure, rather than a mere means of human reproduction'.[4]

Thus marked the beginning of his most celebrated and notorious struggle against forces he had opposed all his life. However, Kemmy found himself in a lonely place, with much of the Limerick clergy, the leadership of the Limerick Labour Party, other political parties and the *Limerick Leader* raging against him.

It resulted in significant hardship, culminating, after a vicious campaign by such advocates as the Christian Political Action Movement – which had targeted him, Mary Robinson, myself and others – in the loss of his Dáil seat in the November 1982 General Election, as I lost my own. Labour's Frank Prendergast won a seat for Labour. There can be little doubt that Kemmy's defeat, as he correctly identified at the time, was a result of this targeted campaign against

him, centring on the use of the abortion issue by his many and varied opponents. Sermons containing anti-abortion rhetoric were widespread in city churches on the Sunday before the election poll. The *Limerick Leader* had run a front-page editorial calling him an 'abortionist' and referring to 'Deputy Kemmy's way of death'.[5] Even the Labour Party, competing for a seat, placed advertisements in local newspapers stating it was opposed to abortion in an effort to distance itself from him.

Jim Kemmy had a lifelong interest in local history and that of the labour and trade-union movement. He published the *Limerick Socialist*, treating readers to extracts from the writings of Connolly, Engels, Larkin, Marx and Conor Cruise O'Brien. He revived an interest in the writings of Kate O'Brien. He edited the quarterly *Old Limerick Journal* and found time to serve in various cultural positions.

He was a generous man. I recall several acts of generosity, including, in 1991, when he was elected Mayor of Limerick, his donation of the full mayoral salary to help offset cutbacks in city contributions to twenty-five local organisations. Toddy O'Sullivan and I were among those who spent time with him during his hospitalisation and his final illness.

In remembering Kemmy, I am minded to recall how his life represents a life built on the best of utopian ideas put into practice. Utopia may never fully exist in reality – it derives its meaning ambiguously from the ancient Greek words for 'no place' and 'good place' – but I ask, if this is not a time ripe for dreaming of utopias, then when would be? Is it not a time for an ethical and sustainable political economy, a time for moral impulse on politics, such as that practised by Jim Kemmy, for we cannot ignore our present circumstances and challenges.

I recall the peace marches of decades ago, the anti-racism meetings, and I am appalled at how the rhetoric of the Cold War has returned, how militaristic our discourse has become. After the financial crash of 2008, we have witnessed the greatest growth of xenophobic extremism in the democratic world, and, as a result of the Covid-19 pandemic, many certainties of preceding decades have been upended, leaving a vacuum which utopian ideals with diverse moral considerations should properly fill. Where now are the marches for peace, the confrontations with the armaments industry?

Drawing on scholarship such as that of Ruth Levitas and Ernst Bloch, it is by questioning the false inevitabilities that we have been handed from which we make our hope, as Jim Kemmy did throughout his life; a practised hope that will enable us to change everything – challenge these assumptions of war and exploitation, upend them, have the courage to propose radical alternatives, to take our first steps with diverse others on a journey of hope. Out of such an alliance of curiosity, intellectual rigour, moral courage and dogged determination, a new ethical, sustainable society can emerge, one which Jim Kemmy sought to realise, and of which we might all be proud, one that promises a future of inclusion, equality and emancipation.

Notes

1   Brennock, Mark, 'Kemmy, passionate worker for the disadvantaged, dies', *The Irish Times*, 26 September 1997.

2   Devine, Francis, 'Jim Kemmy', *Saothar*, Vol. 22 (1997), pp. 14–18.

3   Ibid., p. 16.

4   Ibid., p. 15.

5   Callanan, Brian, *Jim Kemmy: Stonemason, Trade Unionist, Politician, Historian* (The Liffey Press, 2012).

Poet, academic and former chairperson of the Labour Party, Michael D. Higgins is President of Ireland.

SUNSHINE AT LIMERICK JUNCTION

Sarah Moore

It was 1989, the year *Fair City* was first broadcast on RTÉ, and I didn't know what I was doing in Limerick. I remember shivering in a phone box near the Crescent late one Tuesday night in a desolate quest to hear a voice from home and to shelter from the relentless, horizontal rain.

'I hate it here,' I told my friend on the other end, who sounded as distant as an echo. Only a hundred miles from home. But home was Dublin and this was Munster, and I might as well have been on another planet.

Though I was warmly and kindly received by my new employers and colleagues, who were constantly concerned that I was settling in well, the truth is, I was lonely and lost. I had moved from the security of a world I knew so well to a strange city where I didn't know a soul. In conversation I often felt wrong-footed and stupid. Everything seemed different. The smell of the air, the feel

of the rain, the nuances of unknown social rituals. In those early days I was so far outside my comfort zone that each weekend, as soon as I could, I'd dash for the Friday train from Colbert to Heuston. On Sunday nights, en route back to my good job, with a heavy, homesick heart and a bag full of freshly laundered clothes, I'd stand forlornly on that Siberian wasteland that was the platform at Limerick Junction, where it was always raining.

I think of myself back then, fresh from UCD, knowing little or nothing of Ireland beyond the Pale. How unfriendly I must have seemed, rushing back to Dublin every chance I got, the idea of spending even a single Saturday in this place filling me with a special kind of lonely dread.

Then one day a kindly colleague offered me a spare ticket to a weekend rugby match in Limerick. Needless to say, that maiden visit to Thomond Park in the late 1980s was an extremely far, primal cry from the leafy suburbs of Lansdowne Road. Still there was something about the rhythm and the glory and the banter that made me feel I'd stumbled into the beating heart of Munster.

Slowly the pain of homesickness began to ease, and I woke up one day to find I wasn't feeling quite so lost.

I would end up finding plenty of common ground with the people around me and I would meet many soulmates, including the man who is now my husband. But before that, almost without my noticing, little by little the magic of this part of the world had already begun to reveal itself to me.

It might have been harder to see back in 1989, but even then Limerick city was a jewel of a place. I began to stay for more weekends after all, and discovered many wonderful things: The Clare Glens in Murroe with its fairy-tale waterfall, the brilliant Belltable Arts Centre, the gorgeous Granary Library, Gleeson's, Flannery's, The Round House, The Locke. And beyond the city, further west in County Clare, music and dancing in Ennis, fresh bread at Unglert's bakery in Ennistymon. Seafood and surfing at Lahinch, Liscannor and Doolin, barefoot beach-walking at Spanish Point and Miltown Malbay, and the glorious glitter and foam of the wild Atlantic, different from but connected to the Irish Sea of my home coast. My three children were born and have grown up in Limerick, and since then, my old and new homes have grown much closer. It's strange how I used to feel they were so far apart. Dublin will always be my home town, but Munster is home now too. A place where an unsure, lonely girl found her feet, was given her chance, and more than once was afforded the benefit of the doubt.

How fragile my early commitment to this place had been. How close I once was to packing up and leaving for good but for all the hidden magic that gradually began to change my mind. I remember one particular moment – it was on my Sunday trek back to work at UL sometime in the spring of 1990. I hopped off the train at Limerick Junction and as I walked across the platform, something unexpected occurred to me. There were no puddles. There was no rain. The clouds had parted. And the sun had started to shine.

Sarah Moore, Professor of Teaching, Learning and Creative Practice, is an acclaimed novelist and a key member of the UL Creative Writing team. In 2022, she won the London Magazine Short-Story Award.

EMMET BARRY: NOT LOOKING IN

Kathryn Hayes

For over four decades Emmet Barry, a native of Castleconnell, has worked as a groundsman in the University of Limerick. His job has changed a lot over the years. He started work at UL in 1981, when he was twenty-two. All of his work back then revolved around the logistics of PE at Thomond College. 'That was hard going, in fairness,' he says of the job, which involved a lot of heavy lifting of sports equipment. And despite the extent of his current job remit – 340 acres, spanning two counties – Emmet takes it all in his stride. 'I was in charge of edging at one stage for about twenty-five years non-stop. It was mostly up at the running track – you'd be up there for weeks. It could take five or six weeks to do and as soon as you had it done you would have to go back up and start again.'

As one of eleven children who grew up on a farm, outdoor work is a way of life for Emmet. But it's the human connections he's made over the last forty-one years that have become the fondest part of his job. 'I think the most interesting person I've ever met was a man called John Rogg, or "Roggy" as we called him. He worked with us here for a few years. He was a Polish Jew who had been in a concentration camp in Italy during the Second World War and he came over here from England,' recalls Emmet.

'I was only a young fella when I met him and I had loads of questions, and I wanted all the answers. After a while we were like the terrible twins. If John was asked to do painting, I was painting; if John was asked to clean the stream, I was cleaning the stream; if John was asked to move the goalposts, I would move the goalposts. I was his sidekick and I think I just understood him from day one and we just clicked and became great buddies. He had great stories and we were always together. He was a very interesting guy, he told us once about how himself and two guys escaped from the concentration camp in a sewage truck. They were in the forest for three weeks eating berries and they couldn't get the smell of manure off themselves. He was a really lovely man and every day there would be a story.'

Sadly, Roggy passed away in 1994 and Emmet still misses him terribly.

The sixty-three-year-old has fond memories of some of the other well-known characters he worked alongside in UL over the decades: Micheál Bresnan and the porters in Thomond College; David Weldrick and P.J. Smyth in the Sports Arena; the late Walter Alfred, former Mace Bearer and Concierge at Plassey House. 'Walter was so lovely. He was completely unique. He would be out with the Brasso, polishing the door handle and the university plaque. He would always come over talking to you because everyone was the same with Walter, he had great time for everyone.'

And despite being 'hidden' from many of the visiting dignitaries, Emmet and the grounds staff have got to know a number of UL presidents over the years.

'Ed Walsh really loved the grounds, and no matter who he was with he would always come over talking to you and say, "Well done, you're doing a grand job there on the grounds." Don Barry used to come out for his cigarette, and he'd always come over and talk to you too. He appreciated the grounds too, but I think he appreciated his fag more,' Emmet jokes.

Emmet's favourite place to work on campus is on the grounds around Plassey House. 'I love the grounds up around there, but the lads I work with hate it because of all the windows in the White House. They think there's too many people looking out, but I always say to them, "They won't be looking out if you're not looking in!"'

Not shy to express his opinion, Emmet was once invited to share his thoughts on the architect's plans for the new President's House. 'I said it looked like two handball alleys stuck together. I remember the fella behind me gave me a dig to say it out loud and I did, because that was what I thought, so I just said it out.'

Emmet's favourite season on campus is undoubtedly autumn, because of the burst of colours on campus. He believes the campus needs more colour all year round.

'It's a shame there is no variety in the trees they plant. There's no bit of colour. We have the world of lime trees but why not break them up with some copper beech or some lovely maples? Since the first day I started, they are putting down the same green trees. We've a beautiful blue and yellow flower arrangement now for Ukraine, but why can't we have more of those? We have a lot of foreign students and we should have an area for the different nationalities and plants from their countries; a corner for the Chinese and plants from the all the different countries, it would be brilliant.'

Looking forward to his retirement at the end of the year, Emmet has huge praise for the students he has met down through the years. 'The ones we hear the stories about are the ones up on the roof, and they are only a small few. Students are fabulous and they are only all going through life as well, trying to make a few quid and get on, but they're not the ones making the headlines. The wrong ones are making the headlines, as is very much the same in life. I've met some lovely students and they couldn't be nicer.'

Emmet, who lives in Daly's Cross with his wife Maura, a retired school-teacher, has found many personal belongings while working on UL grounds, from watches to wallets to passports. His most rewarding discovery, however, took place off campus one wet Friday evening, when he was in his local shop and a student sped by on a motorbike and unknowingly dropped a folder containing his final year thesis.

'It was soaked so I brought it home to my dad who had an old fire and he dried the whole lot of it, every single page. I brought it in on Monday to one of the porters in the PE building. He knew the student and we got it to him. He was thrilled, because it was his thesis and he was bringing it home to get it typed up and bound. There were hundreds of pages. It had fallen off his bike and he didn't know where he had left it. That was back in 1985 when there was no internet, so he was delighted to get it back as he had no other copy.'

When asked for his advice to students today, Emmet's advice is simple: 'Slow down. You'll get there. Don't panic. There's loads of jobs out there for ye. I often talk to people who worry about their sons and daughters, but they shouldn't. There's plenty of work out there for everyone.'

Emmet Barry has been a member of the UL grounds team since 9 November 1981. Kathryn Hayes is a journalist and a staff lecturer in Journalism and Digital Communication.

ZONE IN AND FOCUS

Donnah Sibanda Vuma

(in conversation with Joseph O'Connor)

I was born in Bulawayo, in Zimbabwe. When I remember, it was heavenly. I had a happy time in school all the way from primary to secondary and went to an all-girls boarding school for a while. My parents ensured we had everything we needed. I excelled at English.

But I was terrible at maths.

There was one particular teacher I remember, Mrs Khoza, who didn't actually teach me, but I loved her. She was very caring, generous, and also glamorous, very stylish! She wore stilettos and a pencil skirt, and most of the teachers were a bit older. She was newly married, very full of life. She just made you feel better when you looked at her; she was like a model. She always said good morning to you. I think we learned a lot from her.

We studied the British A-level curriculum in my school. I loved novels. Two great favourites were *Great Expectations* and *Oliver Twist*. When I was sixteen, I was involved in a protest against human rights abuses and got into a bad situation. I had to go to South Africa, but the problems followed me there. Sometime later, in 2014, I came to Ireland with my children, seeking protection. I thought we would be in the Direct Provision system for a short while, maybe six months. It ended up being seven years.

It was the most difficult and challenging time of my life.

The hardest thing about parenting in the Direct Provision centre is trying to make it a home. For children, getting used to the food. Because you weren't permitted to cook. You think you've failed. You're living in one room, going to the canteen and back, one room, then the canteen, one room, then the canteen; there isn't any personal space. We wake up, we do it again. This is our life now.

If my children had had a tough day, I'd tell them go take a bath. The one luxury I always made sure we had was soap bubbles. I'd say, go in and take a hot bath, try to relax, have some time. And that's what I would do myself. I did a lot of crying in that bathroom.

Sometimes I'd come out and the children would say to me, 'What's the matter, why are your eyes all red?' I'd tell them, don't worry, it's the soap.

You weren't allowed to work and so sometimes you'd think you had failed your children. I had worked in sales and marketing before, for a company retailing office equipment, but I wasn't permitted to work here, or to upskill or study. So, they couldn't have, for example, trainers or internet access. Or books. I'd often think, 'The cost of my safety has come at the price of my freedom.'

People sometimes think Africa is a country. It's not. It's a continent. With hundreds of languages, different cultures, outlooks, traditions. It's hard when you're living in Direct Provision to give your children that sense of values and identity.

The first time I visited the UL campus was with a friend, for a walk. I was mesmerised. My friend said, 'Come on, I'll show you the most beautiful place in Limerick.' It was evening-time – I'll never forget it – we went to the Living Bridge and walked from there down to the Kemmy building. I remember the lights in the pond, all the glass in the buildings. Just magical. Oh my word.

And the next time was to attend someone's graduation ceremony. I wasn't really concentrating. But when it came time for the PhD students to be conferred, I found myself thinking, 'I want to do that one day.' The thought wouldn't leave me. The next morning I said it to Aideen Roche at Doras Luimní (an independent, non-profit, non-governmental organisation working to promote

and protect the rights of people from a migrant background in Ireland). She said, 'Okay. Let's figure it out.'

This was before UL became a Sanctuary University or anything like that. But I made up my mind. I thought, I want an education. So I can better my children's lives. And I want to contribute to society in a meaningful way.

I'm doing the MA in Peace and Development Studies, looking at how effective, or not, aid organisations and NGOs are, and the whole issue of structural development. I'll be able to tell you in a few months' time, when I've finished! I love to read, so I like studying. Then, I intend to do my PhD.

If there was a magic wand that I could wave to change one thing in UL, it would be to get rid of international fees for asylum seekers and people from other countries waiting for a decision on their applications for International Protection. The Sanctuary Scholarship is great, but it only goes so far. I feel it is an important issue that needs to be addressed.

I would say to anyone who is thinking of doing a university degree, it's natural to be a little bit scared. It's new. And it *is* a change. You might be a bit older than is usual, or education might be something you're coming back to after a time. So then, you're worried that 'everyone will be younger than me' or everyone will be smarter. But actually, when you have that bit of life experience you get so very much from education. Focus in on what you want. Zone in and focus. UL, for example, is a very diverse place. You'll be fine. There is so much support and goodwill, advice on childcare and things like that. The supports exist and are there for you. If it isn't available from the university, they'll be able to tell you where to look.

Education to me means knowledge, hope and power. It means a shifting in one's way of thinking and being able to identify one's own worth.

The Mature Access programme at UL is really so wonderful. I'd say, don't be frightened. You can cope. Zone in.

Donnah Sibanda Vuma lives in Clare with her children. The organisation she founded, Every Child is your Child, is a community group dedicated to helping parents living in Direct Provision.

THE STUFF OF DREAMS

Vivienne McKechnie

I'll see you back to the lamp-post. I suppose you can find your
way from there back to Spare Oom and War Drobe?

C.S. Lewis, *The Lion, the Witch and the Wardrobe*

Swans swim silently on the River Shannon
as it flows though the university campus.
They are a constant presence but oblivious
to the students' struggles or successes.
Their separateness a mirror to peer into –
elegantly white in their own world,
a source of inspiration, a touch of beauty.

A heron balances motionless and waits,
watching the water under the wobbly bridge
while people rush or meander back and forth,
each step creating a motion unique to this place.
This living bridge linking Limerick and Clare
lifting and falling under feet from everywhere.

A fox finds a pathway in darkness, moves mysteriously,
a cautious foray, padding past unlit rooms,
seeing only the silhouette of a solitary student studying
or watching warily from the shadows
as party music blares and the black night is lit up like day.

Another world within this world of worlds.
The outside looking in, the inside looking out.

You stand at the entrance on that inaugural morning
fearful of the first footstep, the one taking you
past the black and white chequered wall,
the brown flagged pillars guarding the entrance,
towering high above, enticing and intimidating.
You pause though you are eager to start
yet full of apprehension like all explorers.
You remember reading of Amelia Earhart,
take courage in her bravery, her solo experience –
wanting, like her, to fly across an ocean,
listen to the breath of a new land.
Or venture out of a train into a new universe,
go through the branches and leaves of a forest,
push through all barriers to be there or here.

Then you take that tentative step, like Lucy through the wardrobe –
The reassuring feel of fur coats at first leading her on.
Then more steps take her, and you, into Narnia.
And you too are excited and inquisitive in this strange place
where Aslan could roam or a white queen glide into sight.
Or tales of wizards unfold under the sparrowhawk's wings.
New normalities evolving, wonder full
like the story of Lyra and Pantalaimon's life in Oxford,
daemons for everyone, subtle knives letting the light of other lands in.

A new realm for the imagination as ideas become words.
Books read, thoughts shared, stories created and what emerges
becomes something ethereal, fantastical, different.
All the time you're alert to your surroundings,
to conversations, light changing, movement and magic –
Words weaving together in workshops.

The brain stretched and contracted, pushed and open,
the war drobe door off its hinges as you let the ideas in.

Surrounded by a city yet apart –
each faculty finding its own features.
New faculties finding their way in,
enlarging this universe, this haven, this oasis of creativity.

Though you are often lost in the labyrinth of UL's landscape,
new buildings burgeoning, changing your route map,
you find, like Lucy, that lamppost and the light shining
letting you learn, finally, the way in from the carpark.
Now you watch everything –
always aware of the seasons' changes,

umbrellas opening in rain and snow,
sunshine sometimes shining through clouds,
pillars of light landing on the pillars below.
Here each day is a celebration –
Acceptance of deadlines and discussions
and at night a full moon high in the blue-black sky,
its chalky white light showing the students the way home.

Swallows in summer, miraculous outlines against the sky.
A ladybird landing, dramatically red, wings fanned, ready for flight.
Even a snail's slow slimy crossing is worth noting, something to write about.
Once a bird trapped in the room, frantic wing beats
fighting for freedom, the glass a barrier
till you set him free.
His flight a straight line, a sudden departure.
A distraction to fill a story.

The end is a rush and a swirl and a flash of light as you leave, prepare the
final dissertation.

Afterwards, when it is all over –
you make your way past the pointed pillars,
push through the coats in the musty wardrobe,
moth balls bouncing out as you open the doors
and step back into the ordinary of everyday,
but it too has changed.
Now everything is a little lighter, snow-tinted –
That time fixed forever, eternally present.
The clock set at the same hour, but soundless, the tick tock suspended.
A woman in white waiting at the table which is always set.

A fox forever finding a foothold in your imagination,
his pawprint patterns printed under oak and ash –
her pause for the elusive runner sprinting through the hazel wood.
The moon, full or otherwise, filling the page.

Swans swim silently on rivers elsewhere,
oblivious – yes – but a constant presence.
They are white lights, lanterns in the dark,
echoes of the children of Lir turning and returning,
reverberating through your words, reminding you of Narnia and Earthsea,
of other worlds everywhere, just a thought away,
creating new beginnings – bewitching, beguiling, intriguing –

The magic mystery of creation.
The stuff of dreams.

UL graduate Vivienne McKechnie is a Limerick-based poet and stalwart of the Limerick Literary Festival in Honour of Kate O'Brien. Her first collection is A Butterfly's Wing.

COPYRIGHT, CREDITS AND ACKNOWLEDGEMENTS

Each piece of writing in this book is the copyright property of its author and may not be reproduced or republished without the advance written permission of the author. The selection is copyright of the University of Limerick and the editors. Unless indicated otherwise, all photographs and illustrations in this book are the copyright property of the University of Limerick or of Special Collections, the Glucksman Library, and appear by prior written permission of the copyright owners, for which grateful acknowledgement is made, and may not be reproduced or republished without prior written permission. Photographers (where names are known to the editors) are – front cover: Sean Reidy; pp. ii and iii: DCIM\100 Media; pp. xi, xv and xvi: True Media; p. xviii: Brian Arthur; pp. 22, 28, 46, 50, 52, 65, 68, 77, 80, 87, 119, 173, 178, 232, 233, 250: Alan Place; pp. 36, 60, 62, 98, 111, 248: Sean Curtin; p. 116: Olivia O'Keeffe, UL Library; p. 163: Oisin McHugh; pp. 202 and 204: Diarmuid Greene; p. 225: Liam Burke; pp. 184 and 185: the Alan Martin and L-Pop Archives, Eoin Devereux; pp. 44, 82, 130, 134, 136, 146, 230 and 236: Special Collections, the Glucksman Library. Mícheál Ó Súilleabháin's contribution is excerpted from a keynote address at the world conference of the International Council for Traditional Music, UL, July 2017. The article first appeared in the *Yearbook for Traditional Music*, Cambridge University Press. Earlier versions of Joseph O'Connor's and Sarah Moore's contributions were written for the RTÉ radio programme, *Sunday Miscellany*, recorded live before an audience at the Irish World Academy of Music and Dance, UL, 13 May 2018, produced by Sarah Binchy, as part of the UL Creative Writing Festival. Sindy Joyce's contribution is a lightly edited excerpt from the opening address to the Arts Council conference 'Places Matter', March 2019. Aoife O'Sullivan's and Caoimhe Gaffney's contributions are excerpts from final-year projects undertaken by their authors while students at UL. Aoife's supervisor was Joseph O'Connor; Caoimhe's was Eoin Devereux. The poems by Mary O'Malley and Martin Dyar were commissioned by the UL President's Office and published in *The Irish Times* on 7 July 2018. Conor Lavery's and Keith Brownlie's contribution is a lightly edited extract from 'University of Limerick "Living Bridge": A Design Response to Sensitive Landscape, Ireland', first published in *Structural Engineering International*, February 2011. Grateful acknowledgement is made to the co-authors. The extract from 'This Land Is Your Land', written by Woody Guthrie, is courtesy of TRO Essex Music LTD, and from 'People Get Ready', written by Curtis Mayfield, is courtesy of Sony Music Publishing Ltd.